Lilach Lev Ari

Contemporary Jewish Communities in Three European Cities

I0079744

Lilach Lev Ari

Contemporary Jewish Communities in Three European Cities

Challenges of Integration, Acculturation and Ethnic
Identity

DE GRUYTER
OLDENBOURG

This book was published with the support of *Oranim* Academic College of Education and the *Kantor Centre* for the Study of Contemporary European Jewry at Tel Aviv University.

ISBN 978-3-11-135555-9
e-ISBN (PDF) 978-3-11-069881-7
e-ISBN (EPUB) 978-3-11-069890-9

Library of Congress Control Number: 2021950700

Bibliographic information published by the Deutsche Nationalbibliothek
The Deutsche Nationalbibliothek lists this publication in the Deutsche Nationalbibliografie; detailed bibliographic data are available on the Internet at http://dnb.dnb.de.

© 2023 Walter de Gruyter GmbH, Berlin/Boston
This volume is text- and page-identical with the hardback published in 2022.
Cover image: Ion Jonas using city maps of Antwerp, Paris and Brussels. Map of Brussels and Antwerp: Maxger/iStock/Getty Images Plus; Map of Paris: lasagnaforone/DigitalVision Vectors/Getty Images
Typesetting: Integra Software Services Pvt. Ltd.
Printing and binding: CPI books GmbH, Leck

www.degruyter.com

Preface

The majority of contemporary world Jewry resides in western countries, due to the West's rather hospitable socioeconomic and political circumstances vis-á-vis Jewish presence. Jews in western nations constitute a privileged ethnic minority group. Culturally, professionally and economically they integrate well, even if they remain a distinct ethno-cultural group. However, as such, they are particularly vulnerable to attacks from the underprivileged, who direct their resentment against mainstream society towards Jews.

In the last few decades most European Jews can be defined as 'native-born' that perceive themselves as a distinct national group, which became a minority due to political and social changes in their homeland. Jewish immigrants in Europe comprise more than a quarter of the Jewish population. Jews world-wide prefer to live in large cities that provide opportunities for economic, social and cultural mobility. Within these cities many Jews tend to concentrate in neighborhoods that are appropriate to their socioeconomic status, provide nearby employment opportunities, facilitate social mobility and offer religious services and Jewish organizations.

More than half of French Jewry reside in Paris and almost all Belgian Jews dwell equally in the two largest cities in Belgium, Brussels and Antwerp. The three cities were chosen for study since they are geographically adjacent and can be considered as Francophone western countries. The cities are characterized by their ethnically diverse Jewish communities: Secular, religious, ultra-Orthodox, *Ashkenazi* (parents' origin is from Europe or America), *Sephardi* (parents' origin is from Africa or Asia), native-born and immigrant. Furthermore, Paris is a metropolis and a 'world city,' i.e. a global center of business, politics, culture and technology that has attracted for decades many Jewish migrants, particularly from the Middle East. Brussels is also a world city and serves as the center of the European Union. Due to lack of one homogeneous national Belgian population in the city, Brussels, as the center of the European Union, with its EU institutions is considered cosmopolitan, and attracts many migrants from all over the world, including Israel. Antwerp is unique due to its changing scope and structure of Jewish population, mainly owing to the growing ultra-Orthodox population. Antwerp is also internationally known for its diamond trade, a sector that has been dominated by the large Orthodox Jewish community in the city.

The three cities are somewhat similar in their culture (the usage of French is common, particularly in two of them), but also unique, as they belong to different nation states. They are also characterized by long standing Jewish history of dynamic interactions with local non-Jewish populations, both native-born

https://doi.org/10.1515/9783110698817-202

and migrant, until the present day. All three cities have large and vibrant Jewish communities.

Whereas numerous studies focus upon Jews of the United States, both native-born and migrants, few studies have explored contemporary Jews in Europe. This book contributes to research by focusing on Jewish ethnic identity, integration and acculturation of both native-born and immigrants in three European cities. The need for research on West European Jews has become even more urgent today in view of the current wave of antisemitism, accompanied by numerous violent incidents, including barbaric murders. Evidently, Europe is facing an overall rise in racism and xenophobia. Jews in France and Belgium express increasing interest in immigrating to Israel or to other destinations.

The main contribution of the book is manifest in elaborating on theoretical terms such as minorities and their socio-cultural integration within the majority, community organizations, both formal and informal, religious or secular, ethnic identity and identification. In addition, the book presents analyses of challenges, strengths, vitality, dynamics and continuity of these three Jewish communities, including their native-born, short and long-term immigrants. Common traits as well as differences among the three communities are discussed according to three themes: 1) Integration, segregation and assimilation into the non-Jewish majority; 2) Jewish communal continuity and vitality; 3) Multiple ethnic identity and identification, as well as acculturation.

Furthermore, the usage of mixed methods analysis, quantitative and qualitative, enables the elaboration and explanation of several sociological terms that enhance the reader's understanding of lives of minorities and immigrants in contemporary Western Europe. These terms are related to various dimensions of ethnic identity: Local (assimilative), transnational (with homeland) and diasporic. The book delineates patterns of social integration and acculturation versus segregation, as each group lives in a nation state with different cultures, languages and policies towards minorities and immigrants.

This comprehensive study in two geographically adjacent nation states, necessitated by rising antisemitism and the urge for a thorough, updated study of Jewish identity currently emerging in Europe, may therefore contribute to and enrich ongoing scientific and public discourse regarding similarity and difference between diversified Jewish communities. It will also promote further understanding of Jewish continuity and vitality as well as of social structures which maintain them within the larger non-Jewish host societies.

Accordingly, the potential audience for this book includes scholars of European Jewry in particular and in general, people interested in ethnic identity, integration and acculturation among minorities – both native-born and immigrants –

particularly in large cities. This book also provides data for policy makers regarding: 1) Europe-Israel relationship, from the Israeli and European-Jewish points of view; 2) Minority and majority relationship as well as native-born and immigrants' integration from non-Jewish local or even national aspects; 3) Local community policy and possible cooperation of the three, aimed to strengthen the communities and increase their resilience. It may also serve as a textbook for the many Jewish studies programs in universities in Europe and around the world. The study also targets casual readers, especially Jews, concerned about contemporary Jewish communities, their resilience and strengths vis-à-vis new waves of antisemitism in general, and in Europe, in particular.

The empirical basis for this study includes data collected via closed-ended questionnaires and semi-structured interviews which were conducted during 2017 in the three cities in West Europe. In the course of research, I received assistance in contacting the research population from the Israeli Ministry of Absorption and from its representative organization (The Israeli House) in each city, as well as from local Jewish organizations. I requested local people involved in the community to distribute questionnaires to their Jewish relatives, friends and people in their social networks. The in-depth interviews were conducted primarily by me.

I would like to thank the Kantor Center at Tel Aviv University for enabling me to pursue this study and *Oranim* College, my home base for years, for its constant and significant support. I am grateful to my wonderful editor, Dr. Naomi Belotserkovsky for her great help throughout the writing process. Special thanks to my research assistants in each city, particularly to Dr. Efrat Tzadik, who helped me collect the questionnaires and translate some of the interviews. Special appreciation is due to the editorial team of De Gruyter Publishers for their patience and willingness to publish this book. Finally, and most importantly, my gratitude is extended to all the participants in this study, who spent their time either completing the questionnaires or participating in the interviews, thus giving me the opportunity to learn about their life experiences in their home cities in contemporary France and Belgium.

Contents

Chapter 1
Introduction: Social Migration, Ethnic Identity, Socio-Cultural Integration and Acculturation of Migrants and Ethnic Minorities

1.1 Social Migration: Definition and Theories

Human beings have been migrating since the dawn of history. People moved from place to place for different reasons: Economic, social and political (Castles and Miller, 2009). Migration and its socio-cultural ethnic and racial consequences are extremely influential regarding contemporary politics world-wide: "Never before have political leaders accorded such priority to migration concerns" (Castles et al., 2014: 317).

The United Nations defines international migrants as "persons who are either living in a country other than their country of birth or in a country other than their country of citizenship" (United Nations, 2020: 5). Furthermore, an international migrant has been defined as any person who has changed his or her country of usual residence, distinguishing between 'short-term migrants' (those who have changed their countries of usual residence for at least three months, but less than one year) and 'long-term migrants' (those who have done so for at least one year) (United Nations, 1998: 9–10). In this book I will refer to those who reside in the country less than 15 years as 'short-term' immigrants, whereas 'long-term' immigrants will be those who reside in host country more than 15 years. Terms of immigration were defined on the basis of Chiswick's (1978) dichotomy. In addition, between 13 to 15 years after immigration, large portion of immigrants, particularly those who attained medium to high socio-economic status in their country of origin, achieve a socio-economic status similar both to their previous one and to that of a native-born. These findings are also confirmed in more recent studies among Israelis in the United States (Lev Ari, 2008; Rebhun and Lev Ari, 2010). Indeed, migration has been growing (Koser, 2010; Urry, 2007) to the point of becoming a major social problem, as is the case with many thousands of migrants seeking to enter Europe today. The United Nations' figures point to a significant increase in the number of migrants each year.

Although preliminary estimates suggest that the pandemic (COVID-19) may have slowed down growth in numbers of international migrants by around two million by mid-2020, 27% less than the growth expected since mid-2019, still, in 2020, there were 281 million people living outside their country of origin. In comparison, two decades ago, in 2000, 173 million people emigrated

https://doi.org/10.1515/9783110698817-001

world-wide. Currently, international migrants represent about 3.6% of world population. The largest number of international migrants resided in Europe, with a total of 87 million, whereas northern America hosted the second largest number of migrants, with almost 59 million. Northern Africa and western Asia followed, with a total of nearly 50 million. Nearly half of all international migrants world-wide were women or girls. In 2020, the number of female migrants slightly exceeded male migrants in Europe. Finally, 73% of all international migrants were between the ages of 20 and 64, compared to 57% for the total population (United Nations, 2021).

Technological, political and cultural factors make migration easier today than in the past. Communication and transportation technologies have become more advanced and their costs are continually dropping. Western nations that currently have low birth rates and aging populations have eased the restrictions for migrants to enter and even offer benefits to those with the required attributes. In addition, people's increased level of education today and their openness to the outside world motivate them to try living in another country. Due to all these factors along with the significant growth in migration world-wide, the current era beginning in the 1980s has been dubbed "the age of migration"(Castles and Miller, 2009). Migration is practically unavoidable, forced by the need to flee war, violence, political repression, religious persecution or poverty (United Nations, 2016). It can also be voluntary, as in the case of brain drain, a type of migration that occurs mainly as a result of economic opportunities, including the possibility of job promotion or career change. In this type of migration people seek a better quality of life for themselves and their families in the form of a wider range of economic opportunities, professional advancement, and more opportunities for economic and social mobility than in their country of origin (Favell et al., 2007; Lev Ari, 2008).

Classical theories of migration motivations referred to geographical differences in income, employment and other, mainly economic opportunities. However, in the last few decades, better access to education and information, as well as social capital, have increased people's aspirations and capabilities to migrate. Migration is very complex and motives to migrate are often manifold: It is difficult to separate economic from social, cultural and political incentives for migration. Thus, migration should be seen as the result of interacting macro and micro social structures, such as the world market or interstate relationships versus family ties. The macro and micro levels are linked by 'meso-structures' such as migrant networks, immigrant communities and 'migration industry.' Migration theories can be grouped into two main paradigms of Social Sciences: The functionalist push-pull models and historical-structural, or neo-Marxist theories that perceive migration as a result of capitalism. Today, migration is not just a passive and predictable response to poverty; development processes tend to reinforce migration by increasing capabilities and aspirations to move from one geographical area to another (Castles et al., 2014; Hollifield and Wong, 2015).

In recent decades international migration has also been referred to as 'transnational migration.' This approach places emphasis on the differences between migration in the past and contemporary migration. Transnational migration is a process in which migrants maintain network ties to their past and forge new ties that connect between their society of origin and the place in which they resettle (Basch et al., 1994). The social space of transnational migrants is dynamic and changes, frequently by means of a set of connections and commitments to more than one place (Levitt and Glick-Schiller, 2004). Moreover, these social spaces have more branches and the migrants remain in contact with their national group in different places across the globe as well as with longtime local residents from their ethno-religious group (Levitt and Jaworsky, 2007). Thus, it is not only the migrants themselves who are affected by transnational migration, but also native-born residents are influenced by the flow of people, money and social patterns of norms, values, ideas and identities through spaces. Migrants act simultaneously in different transnational spaces, creating a diverging set of mutual social, economic, cultural and political ties. This process has major influence on the patterns of their integration in the host society and sometimes generates dual loyalty to two countries (Rebhun and Lev Ari, 2010).

In light of this view, migrants are actors in transnational spaces. Their behavior affects not only the patterns of absorption and integration in the host societies, but also relations with the country of origin. This concept of transnationalism poses an alternative to the older bifocal model (departure and arrival) and suggests instead, dual orientation to both host and origin societies. Structural and personal motives for migration may thus be examined as part of a dynamic process where migration is not a final step, but rather an additional move, and a migrant's return to the country of origin or emigrate to a third country is always possible (Lev Ari, 2015; Vertovec, 2010).

Transnational communities used to be called Diaspora, which is a term often used for people displaced or dispersed by force (e.g. Jews), but can be also applied to trading groups or labor migrants. Recently, Diaspora has been used to denote almost any migrant community (Castles et al., 2014). In light of the transnational theory, the term trans-migrant can be used to identify people who participate in transnational communities based on migration (Glick-Schiller, 1999). However, not all migrant communities fit transnational patterns: Some are temporary labor migrants with very few connections with the host society while others are permanent migrants who retain very loose contacts with their homeland (Castles et al., 2014).

Some migrant groups, after their initial integration in a host country or city, develop their own sub-communities or ethnic group, as well as social, cultural and economic organizations: Places of worship, formal and informal educational institutions for their children, media channels and other services. These sub-communities and institutions reflect on their ethnic identity and identification (Castle and Miller, 2009; Castles et al., 2014; Gold, 2016). Ethnic minorities, ethnic identity and identification will be the focus of the next section.

1.2 Ethnic Identity and Identification

Finding a common definition of the concept of *minorities* is very complex. Nevertheless, until a few years ago, a sort of "soft" consensus on the notion of minority prevailed in Europe. A minority was considered a group of citizens of a state, constituting a numerical minority and holding a non-dominant position in that state, endowed with ethnic, religious or linguistic characteristics which differ from those of the majority. However, among the members of 'new minorities' some are citizens of their new home country and are in the process of integration, while others are neither citizens nor assimilated. These differences call for policies regarding their integration and inter-relations with the majority (Plasseraud, 2010). Thus, Jews, for example, constitute mainly an ethnic, native-born minority group in Europe, i.e., a group whose culture and religion is differentiated from that of the majority and thus, liable to experience relative discrimination (Macionis, 1999; Yiftachel, 2001).

Ethnic identity is a concept formed by dynamic day-to-day interactions between migrants and minority groups and the majority group (Portes and Rumbaut, 2001). Although ethnicity is usually seen as an attribute of minority groups, sociologists define ethnicity which everyone has – to some degree. Ethnic identity has a number of components: Sense of group belonging based on ideas of common origin, history and culture (Castles et al., 2014). Ethnic identity is defined as beliefs, values and feelings toward an ethnic group (Rebhun, 2001; Lev Ari, 2013): It is constructed dynamically and continues to develop following changes in the location of the group and the individual and changes according to the social structure of the destination nation or community. Ethnic boundaries are defined and redefined by constant negotiation and are restructured through reciprocal relations between various groups (Lev Ari, 2013). Identity is not constant and can change over time, following psychological changes and diverse situations (Sheffer, 2003). In an era in which people live in the global village, ethnic identity is anchored in a variety of geographic spaces situated beyond national borders. Indeed, ethnic identity has become transnational identity (Glick-Schiller et al., 1992).

Furthermore, transnational-global migration can be associated with multiple identities, which allow migrants to have several ethnic identities at the same time. Another theoretical term in this context is 'hyphenated identity,' namely, dynamic interaction among these multiple identities, which sometimes are apart and sometimes in harmony. The hyphen unites and separates at the same time between the self and the Other. Thus, hyphenated identities could lead to internal contradictions or to feelings of complementation – when each identity complements the other (Hertz-Lazarowits et al., 2010).

Unlike identity which is external to the individual, ethnic identification represents a willful, conscious act on part of the individual. Individuals identify their emotions, their consciousness or their values with the practices of a particular group. In order for identification to constitute a genuine process of establishing or changing identity, three main elements are required: A formal element expressing a genuine desire to belong to the group with which the individual identifies, an independent element according to which the individual must adopt the group identity as the group defines it, and a practical element in which the individual must put group actions into practice (Sagi, 2002). Ethnic identification is the outer and behavioral expression of identity, and its components are manifested through expression of opinions and viewpoints and through actual behavior linking the individual to a particular ethnic group. Ethnic identification is the genuine expression of connection to an ethnic or religious group (DellaPergola, 2011a). Migrants and members of ethnic groups who have new experiences and find themselves in new situations make a choice regarding what they identify with, what parts of their identity they wish to preserve and what parts they would like to change (Featherstone, 2000; Ellemars et al., 1999).

In this context, diasporic identity is one in which values, norms and narratives of the country of origin are preserved in the host country and may sometimes conflict (Lev Ari and Cohen N., 2012; Lev Ari, 2013). More than identities of other ethnic groups, diasporic identities are inflexible in that they are based on initial values such as biological ties due to the decision to preserve "pure ethnicity." This identity is also based on symbolic and cultural components, anchored in the history of groups that live outside their native lands and still "live" within the thoughts and memories of the group members. This type of identity enables migrants to feel at home away from home (Sheffer, 2003). Diasporic identity underscores the otherness of the migrants as manifested in their identification with their homeland, to the point that they continue to nurture their ties with their country of origin while at the same time persist with the process of assimilating into their new home (Kivisto, 2001). These ties can occur in a number of areas: Family, economic, social, organizational, religious and political. Members of a diasporic group are partners to the historical heritage of their homeland and feel a sense of identity and solidarity with it (Rebhun and Lev Ari, 2010).

Another component of immigrants' and ethnic minorities' integration in the host society is their social relationship with family, friends and their communities – this will be the focus of the next section.

1.3 Social Networks and Community

One of the central concepts in the social integration of migrants and other ethnic groups is social networking. Social networks are sets of links between the absorbing country and the country of origin based on kinship, socialization and ethnic or national origin, and are achieved by means of family relations, socialization and common country of origin (Rebhun and Lev Ari, 2010). These networks help migrants and ethnic minorities cope with the economic, cultural and social hardships of their integration. The size of these social networks is determined by the number of people in a given group. The members can be loosely or tightly bound to one another. In tightly bound networks the individual has frequent contacts and common identities and activities with the other members of the network. These are known as multiplex networks. In loosely bound networks the individual is connected with other people in the network, on the basis of a single activity (uniplex networks). Tightly bound networks are related to the number of connections within the group. If all the members of a network are connected to each other, the network is very tightly bound (Avenarius, 2012). Social networks exert major influence on various aspects of migration (Boyd, 1989). They help maintain ties to the country of origin and to relatives and friends at home (Avenarius, 2012; Vertovec, 2007). Indeed, already at the beginning of the migration process, as soon as these migrants start thinking about their desire to migrate, these networks play an important role (Ferro, 2006). They also decrease the risks involved in leaving the country of origin (Massey et al., 1993). Social networks also affect the results of migration, whether the migration efforts are successful (remaining and becoming integrated into the new society) or they fail (returning to the country of origin, failing to integrate, feelings of alienation). Integration in the host country goes hand in hand with pulling up roots and replanting them in the new environment. Social networks help individuals reconcile with the integration process (Geoffroy, 2007) by creating social solidarity. In some cases, social networks provide minority groups of migrants with financial help for housing, information and help in finding work, social assistance and emotional support (Avenarius, 2012; Koser, 2010). Such networks can be based on diasporic and transnational relationships (Rebhun and Lev Ari, 2010). According to transnational theory, these social ties can be found in diverse geographic and social spaces (Rebhun and Lev Ari, 2010; Lev Ari, 2008; Glick-Schiller et al., 1995; Vertovec, 1999, Vertovec, 2010). Social networks, whether formal or informal, are built mainly after the initial integration stages into economic, social and cultural systems and are likely to provide future support for the migrants and their descendants as an ethnic minority group (Rebhun and Lev Ari, 2010). This is because in contemporary international migration, migrants are not unequivocally cut off from their countries of origin. The media, the internet and social networks help reduce feelings of alienation and difference (Sheffer, 2003).

Nevertheless, the experience of emigration from the country of origin and integration into the country of destination is not so simple. Migrants' tendencies toward social separation as opposed to assimilation and their ties to their homeland (transnationalism) have an impact on their and their descendants' future integration. Migrants who are active from the transnational perspective usually tend toward separation from the majority society (Christiansen, 2004). Haug et al. (2007) described three social circles of integration into the host culture that help understand the process involved in feeling at home in a new place. The first circle is the inner circle comprising the home (family), the church (religion) and the school (education). This circle is legally open to strangers. The second circle consists of public spaces shared by locals and migrants, such as shops and markets. The third circle is that of cultural events and traditions that are usually reserved for locals. Migrants and minorities have various reciprocal relations with local native-born. It takes time for them to become integrated into all the circles, and some only become integrated into certain ones. Processes of inclusion in the host or majority society are manifested in the social networks, in the educational, health and financial systems and in how the new migrants obtain rights as local residents. Nevertheless, there is also exclusion not only as far as place of residence is concerned, but also with respect to other social processes, such as racism, xenophobia and prejudice (Schuster, 2005). For this reason, immigration and minority policy in country of residence affects most areas of life: Institutions with which the individual comes into contact, social and family life, education and other factors (Hannam et al., 2006).

Social networks are related to the term 'community,' which has multiple social, historical and psychological meanings (Dinnie and Fisher, 2020). Community is broadly defined as a set of social relationships, emotional closeness, shared sentiments and beliefs, and physical or geographical proximity (Newby,

2013). Furthermore, community also draws on concepts such as locality or neighborhood interests and hobbies, nationality, ethnicity, identity and lifestyles. The term community can describe different sets of social relations such as place, identity, institutions, politics, technology – of various levels and sizes, which are linked spatially, physically and psychologically in a range of ways, and which are multiple and overlapping. There is also a feeling, or 'sense of community.' In an imagined community social bonds do not have to be constantly reenacted; what is important is that people believe that they exist (Dinnie and Fisher, 2020). The imagined community is associated with comfort, security and a sense of belonging, of being 'at home' (Bauman, 2001).

Hence, the contemporary world becomes one in which ethnicity is not disappearing, but rather one where post-modern individuals typically live through personal multiple identities in a pluralized world. The term 'imagined community,' coined by Anderson (cited in Lev Ari et al., 2003), means that membership in this community is by self-definition rather than by personal acquaintance though what is shared by all members of the community; "in the minds of each lives the image of their communion" (Eriksen, 1993: 99).

Belonging to an ethnic community based on religion can serve as a form of extended family, primarily for migrants, and as a setting for ethnic activity and economic support. Being a member of a religiously based community preserves ethnic identity and identification in the relationship between the majority community in which the migrants or minority groups live and their transnational ties to their homeland (Rebhun, 2014).

Some migrants, particularly in their initial phases of their integration in the host society, tend to cluster together in certain neighborhoods to maintain their culture. However, they are not excluded from citizenship, political participation, and opportunities for social and economic mobility, for example, people of South European background in France and Belgium (Castles et al., 2014). By establishing their own neighborhoods and distinctive use of private and public places (Castle and Miller, 2009; Castles et al., 2014; Gold, 2016), migrants also play a significant role in communities' structure. Furthermore, in a globalized world, "identity and community often serve as a focus of resistance to centralizing and homogenizing forces" (Castles and Miller, 2009: 40).

Apart from assistance migrants receive from social networks, family and community, their cultural assimilation into their host countries is extremely complex and requires various strategies that migrant and minority groups use differently on the road to acculturation, as discussed in the next section.

1.4 Acculturation and Cultural Integration

Acculturation is a term that describes the encounters between different ethno-cultural groups and the cultural and psychological changes that take place within the members of each group. As a result of these encounters (Berry, 1997; Berry, 2005) group members arrive at an intercultural intersection which also has the potential for conflict and which produces the need for negotiation in order to achieve results to which both cultures can adapt. Group level acculturation necessitates changes in social structures and cultural customs, while acculturation on the individual level requires behavioral changes. The acculturation process is likely to continue for many years until the groups reach some form of mutual cultural assimilation.

In addition to immigration countries such as the United States and Canada, the notion of acculturation has recently gained importance also in Europe. The colonial past of many European nations has resulted in the emergence of multiple cultures, and the relations between different cultural groups and their adaptation to one another need to be examined. Globalization has reinforced intercultural ties between the native-born residents of these national states and migrants, refugees or temporary residents. Both long-term residents and newcomers share mutual interest in preserving their original cultures, yet within the multicultural encounter they must adapt to the changes presented by each new cultural group (Berry, 2005).

Berry (2001; Berry, 2005) described four possible strategies for assimilation and acculturation based on individuals' attitudes toward the acculturation process and on their actual behavior, exhibited in day-to-day intercultural encounters with the majority. Obviously, not every host culture provides complete freedom of choice when it comes to acculturation. Moreover, the acculturation process also entails individual preferences in the equation between maintaining one's original culture and ethnic identity and choosing the broader culture and other ethno-cultural groups. One strategy is integration. Applying this strategy, migrants are interested in preserving the culture from which they came while maintaining daily ties with the members of the other culture. Another strategy is separation, in which the members of the cultural group identify with their original culture and are not interested in contact with the other culture, preferring to live in an environmental bubble of sorts (see also Lev Ari, 2008: 101). The third strategy is assimilation. Using this strategy, the members of the cultural group are not interested in preserving their original culture and seek ties and contact with other cultures. The final strategy is marginalization, in which the members of the ethno-cultural group are neither interested in their original culture (usually due to being coerced to lose it), nor in adopting the culture of the host society (usually due to exclusion or discrimination).

Based on Berry's model (1997; Berry, 2001; Berry, 2005), Cohen E. H. (2011) proposed eight possible assimilation strategies for ethno-cultural migrant groups. Cohen's model refers to migrants' attitudes toward three reference groups: The host culture, their country of origin's culture, and the ethno-cultural group of their co-migrants in the host culture, namely their diasporic group (Lev Ari and Cohen N., 2012: Rebhun and Lev Ari, 2010). These strategies are: a) group assimilation, in which migrants maintain positive attitudes toward all three reference groups; usually, these are voluntary migrants who resemble the members of the host culture; b) nostalgic separation, in which the group members have negative attitude toward the host culture but positive and nostalgic attitude toward the other two reference groups; c) individual assimilation, in which the members of the migrant group have negative attitude toward their co-migrants in the host culture, but positive attitude toward the other two reference groups; d) individual nostalgic separation, in which the group members have positive attitude toward their country of origin and negative attitudes toward the other two reference groups; e) group acculturation, a pattern marked by positive attitudes toward the host culture and negative attitudes toward the culture of the country of origin, yet at the same time positive attitudes towards their co-migrants from their country of origin; f) group separation, in which the migrants maintain positive attitude toward their co-migrants and negative attitude toward the other two reference groups, a characteristic of minorities who have experienced exclusion in the host country; g) assimilation that characterizes migrants who are interested in becoming integrated into the host culture and in differentiating themselves from the culture of their country of origin and from their ethno-cultural group; and finally, h) marginalization, which characterizes migrants who hold negative attitudes toward all three reference groups (Cohen E. H., 2011; Lev Ari and Cohen N., 2018).

The choice of an acculturation and assimilation strategy is to a large extent also dependent upon the host society and its discourse. In other words, assimilation is possible in societies that espouse multiculturalism by social acceptance, multicultural values, lack of prejudice toward migrants, positive responses to different cultural groups and even a sense of attachment to, or identification with the absorbing society (Berry, 2001; Cunningham and Heyman, 2004). Moreover, migrants' experiences are influenced by other variables, among them socioeconomic status, outward appearance and similarity to members of the host culture, gender and age (Rebhun and Lev Ari, 2010; Lev Ari, 2008; Vertovec, 2007). For example, migrants who come from cultures that are similar to those of the host society report on easier assimilation compared to those whose culture of origin differs drastically from that of the destination society (Berry, 1997). The size of the migrant community or of any ethnic group also affects the cultural patterns of its members; larger groups have greater internal and external impact, while in smaller groups family is more important to the members' culture (Lev Ari, 2008).

In the next section I will describe main migration flows after World War II to Europe in general, and to France and Belgium – in particular. These migration flows brought many Jews to France and Belgium and it is important to discuss policy trajectories in these two countries regarding immigrants, who later became ethno-cultural residents, in general, and Jews – in particular.

1.5 World-Wide Jewry: Between Privileged Minorities and Antisemitism

1.5.1 Jews as Urban Minorities: Dynamic Patterns of Identity

The history of the Jewish people in the modern era is charged with significant migration processes that have resulted in radical changes in its demographic and cultural centers.[1] Jews in western nations constitute a privileged ethnic minority group. Although most minority groups suffer from one form of discrimination or another, some are a 'privileged' ethnic minority: They have social and cultural rights in the country in which they live, and their socio-economic status is high. One prominent example of a privileged minority group is that of American Jews, who have 'become white' over the generations (Brodkin, 1998). These Jews suffered for years from discrimination and racism, but following their move to the suburbs – a process that began after World War II – and after improving their level of education, they experienced upward mobility from the working to the middle class, similarly to Poles, Irish and Italians (Brodkin, 1998; Horowitz, 2008).

Thus, Jews generally integrate well into the society in which they live from the social, cultural, professional and economic perspectives, even if they remain a distinct ethno-cultural group. As such, they are particularly vulnerable to attacks from the underprivileged, who direct their resentment of mainstream society towards Jews (Alidadi et al., 2012; Ben-Rafael, 2017).

Most Diaspora Jews can be defined as native-born minorities, which perceive themselves as a distinct national group that became a minority due to political and social changes in their homeland (Barak, 2006). Immigrants comprise more than a quarter (27%) of the Jewish population in Europe (Graham, 2018).

---

1 World-Wide Jewry in the title refers to Diaspora Jews, not including those residing in Israel.

Most Jews in the world today, both native-born and immigrants (76%) are concentrated in fifteen to seventeen metropolitan regions and large cities (Rebhun and Lev Ari, 2010; DellaPergola, 2017). Jews prefer to live in large cities that provide opportunities for economic, social and cultural mobility. Within these cities, Jews tend to concentrate in neighborhoods that are appropriate to their socioeconomic status, provide nearby employment opportunities, facilitate social mobility and offer religious services and Jewish organizations (DellaPergola, 2011a; DellaPergola and Sheskin, 2015). Furthermore, in 2019 more than half (53.4%) of world Jewry lived in only five metropolitan areas. These five areas – including the main cities and vast urbanized territories around them – were Tel Aviv, New York-Newark-Jersey City, Jerusalem, Haifa, and Los Angeles-Long Beach-Anaheim. Two-thirds (66.6%) of world Jewry lived in the five previously mentioned largest areas plus the following six: Miami and Ft. Lauderdale-Pompano Beach, Washington-Arlington-Alexandria, Chicago-Naperville-Elgin, Philadelphia-Camden-Wilmington, Paris, and Boston Cambridge-Newton. In 2019, the 19 largest metropolitan concentrations of Jewish population, each with 100,000 Jews or more, encompassed 75.8% – over three quarters – of all Jews world-wide (DellaPergola, 2020a).

These metropolises are also known as "world cities" or "global cities." The term "world cities" originated in the 18th century; research interest in world cities increased during the second half of the 1990s. World cities are global centers of business, politics, culture and technology. They are the product of global post-industrial economy and constitute the core of post-industrial society. Kipnis describes these cities as "spatial, centralized and polarized entities that serve as the gates through which national economies enter and exit global economy. These large cities situated at the top of the economic, social and cultural hierarchies serve as entry thresholds to high-level functions and services" (Kipnis, 2009: 230).

In the past, shared values constituted the most dominant component of Jewish identity among Jews world-wide. Yet Jewish identity has changed and has become more individualistic. Membership in Jewish communities in the Diaspora is voluntary. Community members express their sense of Jewishness even if they do not feel that religious beliefs and practices are pertinent to them. For these Jews, being Jewish is important. They are proud of their identity and feel comfortable in their Jewishness. In these communities, Jewish identity is part of, though not in place of, other identities (Medding et al., 1992).

In general, Jewish identity and identification find expression in various contexts: Religious, ethnic, cultural, communal, social, historic and folklorist. Some Diaspora Jews see their identity and identification in the context of being part of Jewish history, while others see it in belonging to Jewish organizations.

In an attempt to simplify this complexity, DellaPergola (2011a) described four possible patterns of attachment to Jewish identity and identification, as well as to a sense of Jewish peoplehood. The first is the *normative-traditional* pattern. Jews who follow this pattern express their identity openly and maintain beliefs, values and norms while conforming to Jewish customs and ceremonies. These Jews accept the authority of their community rabbis and commit themselves to the norms and values that produce a sense of belonging to the community. Another mode of Jewish identity and identification is *ethno-communal.* Jews belonging to this group maintain predominantly Jewish associative networks, in which in-group communication entails spontaneous and not necessarily Jewish-religious content. In this pattern there is no need for religious authority or for defined boundaries to preserve norms, behavior and values. Jews in this group may refer to themselves as secular and use many symbols deriving from the non-Jewish environment while preserving several traditional Jewish customs. The next pattern of Jewish identity and identification is the *cultural residue* pattern. Jews conforming to this pattern express interest in tradition, Jewish history and Jewish culture and even are to some extent involved in Jewish cultural activity, yet in general they are not affiliated with any of the religious streams of Judaism or with Jewish organizations. Their Jewish identity is relatively weak and manifested in occasionally expressed intellectual or emotional interest. The fourth mode of Jewish identity and identification is defined as *dual or none.* This group includes individuals that cannot be assigned to any of the above three categories. The group is characterized by weakened Jewish identification alongside identity and identification with other religions, ethnic groups or communities that are not Jewish (DellaPergola, 2011a).

Although Jews world-wide mostly reside in large cities and enjoy liberal atmosphere and inclusion, one cannot ignore rising antisemitism in the last decades, even, or maybe particularly in western countries, usually considered multicultural. In the next section I will define the general terms: 'Old' and 'new' antisemitism.

1.5.2 Antisemitism: 'New' and 'Old'

Antisemitism in the most simplified caption is a negative perception of Jews. Perceptions of antisemitism imply that some kind of phenomenology exists exterior to those who report about it. Clearly, any person or group of persons tend to report their perceptions of that phenomenology through the lens of their own characteristics, experiences, and – admittedly – biases. Jews' prevalent status as a minority in society as a whole, typically generated parallel positions of Jews versus the hegemonic others in different places. The theory that Jewish history and society might be explained by different local circumstances and did not share some fundamental commonality could lead to the conclusion that there never was and there could not be one antisemitic syndrome. According to this point of view, each local antisemitic manifestation should be judged separately on the merits of the particular civilization within which it occurred (DellaPergola, 2020b; see also Graham, 2018).

Antisemitism has various definitions. Classical antisemitism is defined as beliefs that Jews are bad in nature and cause disasters to their 'host' societies. Furthermore, antisemitic myths accuse Jews of controlling banks and businesses, and associate the practice of discrimination against Jews with racism and. Recently, 'new antisemitism' is embedded in the political left, the political right and radical Islam. 'New antisemitism' denies the rights of Jews to belong to the family of nations (Ben-Rafael, 2017). Another alternative term to antisemitism – allosemitism – is perceived by Bauman (1998) as an explanatory category for representations of Jews and Judaism. This new term encompasses both *Judeophobia* and antisemitism. Postmodern society is becoming multicultured, and thus Jewishness melts into various identity claims and forms which will eliminate antisemitism in the future (Bauman, 1998).

Whereas antisemitism may be considered a factor exogenous to the Jewish collective, its precondition and raison d'être from the beginning was the existence of some kind of corporate Jewish entity. This required consciousness of such an entity on both sides – the perpetrators and those who were the target of hostility. For the antisemitic act or expression to cause offense, damage or uneasiness to Jews, Jews themselves had to be aware of that offensive intention. This implied the existence of a corporate identification among individuals targeted by the offense. Jewish perceptions of negative attitudes by others were therefore integrally intertwined with collective Jewish identity formation and awareness. Israel's independence in 1948 as a declaredly Jewish state – conceptually a filiation of nineteenth-century idealist nationalism but also an expression of long-held sentiments and dreams by Diaspora Jews – engendered a new, hostile argumentative layer. Even more significantly than the independence of Israel, the June 1967 war, with the occupation of Palestinian territories, commenced a new anti-Israeli outlook, which also abundantly drew on several pre-existing anti-Jewish concepts. The multiple ideological foundations of antisemitism did not only include numerous potential strands but also contradictions. These, in turn, profoundly shaped Jewish perceptions of antisemitism. Contemporary antisemitism typology thus comprises a coalescence of several modes of locked modernizations. Each brand of antisemitic outlook is anchored in history and – alone or in combination with others – represents the elective, self-sufficient, and self-perpetuating source of inspiration for different contemporary perpetrators (DellaPergola, 2020b).

During the past 50 years, *Judeophobia* was often downplayed, partly because in its classical form it really had declined. Long-established prejudice against Jews in the West was rarely felt in spheres like housing, education, private economic life or public employment. There was also relatively little discrimination in culture, the media, or politics. On the contrary, Diaspora Jews in the West (especially in the United States, Britain, and France) had ample reason to feel empowered. However, these successes have come at a price. 'New' antisemitism, full of envy and resentment towards Jews who have "made it," lashes out with special vehemence at anything which reflects "Jewish power" and influence, all-too-often perceived through the lenses of classical conspiracy theories. In its insistence that this Jewish empowerment is intrinsically corrupt and illegitimate, such Jew-hatred, frequently directed at Israel, is really old wine in new bottles (Wistrich, 2015).

In the next section I will focus on Jews in Europe and their patterns of integration and ethnic identity, as a result of inter-relations with the majority, primarily in the last four decades.

1.6 Jews in Contemporary Europe: Between Individual, Collective and National

1.6.1 From Colonialism to Resettlement: Policy towards Immigrants and Ethnic Minorities in Europe after World War II

After the end of World War II, international migration changed regarding its directions and characteristics. While for centuries Europeans migrated outward through conquering, colonizing and settling in lands abroad, in the second half of the 20th century people immigrated to Europe (Castles et al., 2014), including Jews to France and Belgium; they constitute a significant portion of the present study.

Due to decolonization, demographic change, rapid economic growth and the creation of the European Union, Europe became a major global migration host. West European countries attracted increasing number of immigrants from former colonies and countries located in the European periphery. While most of these countries do not perceive themselves as immigration societies, the rates of immigrants exceed those of the USA. From 1945 to the early 1970s, the main economic strategy of large-scale enterprises was to invest and expand production in the existing highly developed countries. As a result, large numbers of migrant workers were recruited and employed from less developed countries in the Mediterranean region, among others. The end of this phase was marked by the oil crisis of 1973. France, Belgium, Germany, Luxembourg and the Netherlands signed the Schengen Agreement in 1985. By doing so, they committed themselves to hasten the creation of border-free Europe, in which European citizens could migrate freely among these countries. In the mid-nineties more countries joined this agreement, creating a new class of 'Schengen citizens' (Castles et al., 2014).

After World War II, France established an *Office National d'Immigration (ONI)* to organize recruitment of workers from South Europe, as a solution for post war labor shortages. By 1970 almost two million workers and their families arrived as seasonal agricultural workers mainly from Spain and Portugal. In addition, France experienced large-scale spontaneous immigration from its former colonies in the Maghreb (Algeria, Morocco and Tunisia). Migration from Algeria was regulated by bilateral agreements, which accorded Algerian migrants, including Jews, a unique status. Moroccans and Tunisians, by contrast, were admitted through *Office National d'Immigration (ONI)*, which was established by France in order to recruit workers from Southern Europe, since 1945. The policy was to solve postwar labor shortages. These immigrants were mostly men but with increasing proportions of women in later years. Non-European immigrants in France were mostly channeled to the lower levels of socio-economic status employments. Furthermore, most labor migrants to Western European countries up to the 1970s were workers with low skill level, a new second generation, who were born to foreign-born immigrants; they experienced a different pattern of social mobility. These young people have generally received their education in the host countries and thus have higher educational attainment – compared with their parents, although less than native-born youngsters (20–29) without migration background. Part of the explanation for this gap stems from their parents, first-generation migrants who had low educational attainment (Castles and Miller, 2009; Castles et al., 2014).

The Muslim population in France (traditionally estimated at around six million) may already have reached the eight million mark. It is easily the largest such concentration in the EU, constituting around 12% of the total French population. Like most of France's Jews, since the 1950s, Muslims immigrated principally from the country's ex-colonies in the Maghreb – Algeria, Tunisia and Morocco. This Muslim population has been reinforced by coreligionists from former West African French colonial possessions as well as from Turkey and Iran (Wistrich, 2015).

Classical immigration countries such as the United States, Canada and Australia encourage immigrants to settle permanently and become citizens, thereby assimilating into the host society. Governments that recognize permanent settlement also tend to accept some degree of long-term cultural difference and, in turn, to grant minorities cultural and political rights, although since 9/11 many democracies have to some extent retreated from multiculturalism. Some immigrants assimilate more easily than others, due to abundant social capital and resemblance to the majority of the host population. Others tend to cluster in specific neighborhoods and maintain their original culture.

Another group of host-countries, among them France and the United Kingdom, are former colonial powers that admit immigrants who are already citizens at the time of entry and are less receptive to immigrants from other, non-colonial countries. In most cases, these host countries allow permanent immigration and family reunification. In France, the 1789 Revolution established equal individual rights for all in order to include migrants and other ethnic minorities as equal political subjects. Thus, the government demands individual cultural assimilation of immigrants who receive civil rights. According to this policy, immigrants should become citizens and then will enjoy equal opportunities. Reality, however, is different, as people of non-European birth (whether citizens or not) experience social exclusion and discrimination. Minorities have been segregated in inner-city areas, and offered low-status insecure jobs (Castle and Miller, 2009; Castles et al., 2014).

Similarly to France, in the aftermath of World War II, Belgium was facing serious difficulties in recruiting labor for coal production. Domestic recruitment dried up, forcing authorities to look to foreign labor. Starting with Italy in 1946, Spain (1956), Greece (1957), Morocco (1964), Turkey (1964), Tunisia (1969), Algeria (1970) and Yugoslavia (1970), the government pursued several bilateral agreements. When a crisis struck in the 1960s, these immigrant workers left to find employment in other industries. In the early 1960s, when the demand for labor was still strong, the Ministry of Justice stopped strict application of legislation-governed immigration. New laws were passed to control the granting of work permits in order to regulate the flow of immigrants into the country, in line with economic needs. Since labor migrants were considered temporary guests by policy makers, there was no comprehensive plan to improve their integration in the early years. Only at the beginning of the early eighties were new policies for integration planned and implemented, due to difficulties and conflicts which appeared among these immigrants, particularly from Morocco and Turkey (Florence and Martiniello, 2005; Timmerman et al., 2017).

European unity was to have an important effect on the immigrant question in Belgium, dividing immigrants into two categories: One, in the supranational political sphere of Europe, and the other, composed of what was referred to as third-country nationals, i.e. from non-member countries. The first category enjoyed many legal rights aimed at encouraging equality of treatment between nationals and foreigners, while the second group faced various forms of legal discrimination. As in other European countries, all new immigration of foreign workers was halted in Belgium in 1974, but this did not succeed in stopping immigration. In fact, Belgium has never ceased to be a country of immigration, although immigration is to a lesser extent than before. Immigration since 1974 has changed, especially with regard to the types of immigration and the national origins of the migrants. Many of these immigrants settled permanently, changing the ethnic structure of Belgium's industrial areas. In Belgium, since the early 1980s, the major social fact of migration has become increasingly politicized. The fear that Europe would be invaded by citizens from poorer countries has rapidly spread. Issues linked to cohabitation between "native" Belgians and immigrant ethnic communities have increasingly raised problems of crime, drugs, unemployment, school failure and insecurity (Florence and Martiniello, 2005).

The Belgian federal government has the executive power over migration, citizenship and equal opportunities policies. The State Secretary of Asylum, Migration and Social Integration is since 2008, in charge of policies regulating the entry, the stay and the removal of foreigners, as well as the reception of asylum seekers. The Belgian federal government also has a Minister of Equal Opportunities, in charge of policies against discrimination on the basis of various social categories like gender, sexual orientation, disability, age and ethnic origin. The most important institution with regards to equal opportunities is the Centre for Equal Opportunities and Opposition to Racism. Beyond institutions categorically directed towards immigrants and minorities, it is important to note that diversity has become a widespread policy objective across various policy domains. In 2006, the presidents of all Federal and Programmatory Public Services signed a Diversity Charter to fight discrimination and to promote diversity in the training, selection and recruitment in these public services (Saeys et al., 2014).

After reviewing policy trajectories towards immigrants and minorities in Europe, particularly in France and Belgium, the next section will present recent findings, from the *last decade*, with regard to antisemitism in Europe. These findings reflect some deviation from the multicultural policy towards minorities and immigrants, which was rather prevalent after World War II and beyond in France and Belgium – in general, and towards Jews – in particular.

1.6.2 Recent Antisemitism in Europe (France and Belgium Included)

The Council of Europe has sounded the alarm over growing racism and violence against minorities and NGOs in Europe, fueled by ultra-nationalism, antisemitism, and anti-Muslim hate. Coronavirus-inspired antisemitic expressions constitute forms of traditional hatred towards Jews and of conspiracy theories. So far, these accusations appear to be promoted mainly by extreme rightists, ultra-conservative Christian circles, Islamists, and, to a minor extent, by the far-left, each group according to its narrative and beliefs – such as different conspiracy theories as well as the image of the Jew as the cause of diseases. During 2019 there was a rise of 18% in major violent cases compared to 2018 (456 cases in 2019, compared to 387 in 2018), seven Jews and non-Jews were killed during antisemitic attacks, and a rise has been noted in most other manifestations, in most countries. At least 53 synagogues (12%) and 28 community centers and schools (6%) were 15 attacked. There was also an increase in life-endangering threats (47%) and in attacks on private properties (24%) (Kantor Center, 2020).

Jews in Europe perceive antisemitism in a different manner when compared by states. Jews in Britain and Italy feel less attacked compared with those residing in France and Belgium. These differences are embedded in each community's structure (along, of course, with local policy towards minorities) – whether native-born or immigrants. Whereas in France North African immigrants are the majority among the Jewish community, Belgian Jews, both from Antwerp and Brussels are native-born (Ben-Rafael, 2017). According to a 2018 FRA (European Union Fundamental Rights Agency, 2019) report, 41% of Jews aged 16–34 have considered emigrating from Europe because of antisemitism over the last five years. Antisemitism as the main factor pushing for emigration, might be enhanced by the perceptions regarding governments' mostly ineffectual responses and efforts to eliminate antisemitism (Kantor Center, 2020).

Furthermore, the FRA 2018 survey which covered nine EU Member States (DellaPergola, 2020b), among them France and Belgium, the focus of the present study, indicates some important findings regarding perceptions of antisemitism among Jews. Perceiving antisemitism as an important issue in society ranged between a low of 56% in Denmark and a high of 95% in France. Thus, it clearly demonstrates how much more sensitive Jews are than others when assessing antisemitism and the environment within which it develops. France and Belgium possess some of the strongest perceptions of antisemitism, along with higher proportions of Muslims among the total population, either first-generation immigrants or second-generation local-born younger adults. Regional variation patterns imply the significant involvement of territorially diverse perceptions among resident Jews. Patterns of variation apparently derive from long term religious, cultural, and sociopolitical differences between countries or even cutting across countries – as may be the case in Belgium, Spain, Italy, or the UK. Another determinant may be more recent events such as the quantity of non-European immigration into Europe and the percentage of foreigners, especially Muslims, among the total population. Finer regional distinctions, country by country, and by regions within countries are a matter for further data processing and analysis (DellaPergola, 2020b).

After presenting the current situation regarding antisemitism in Europe, the next two sections describe findings from previous studies which reflect dynamic changes in identity among Jews as constant interactions with the majority.

1.6.3 Jews in Contemporary Europe: Changing Boundaries of Integration and Identity

In spite of the unifying project and process, Europe is much more politically fragmented than the US, making it more difficult to create a homogeneous Jewish population database. However, in recent years the EU concept and ideal finds itself under major stress; the 2016 UK Brexit referendum is only one of its symptoms. Disagreements about migration policies facing large Muslim population have increased in different European locations; they reflect the unsolved dilemma of defining Europe's own cultural identity and geopolitical boundaries. Jewish population decrease continued, reflecting emigration, an overwhelming excess of Jewish deaths over Jewish births, high intermarriage rates, and low rates of Jewish identification among the children of intermarriages (DellaPergola, 2020a).

At the beginning of 2019, the world's Jewish population was estimated at 14,707,400. Europe, including the Asian territories of the Russian Federation and Turkey, accounted for over 9% of world Jewry. The Jewish population in Europe, estimated at 1,340,200 in 2019, is increasingly concentrated in the western part of the continent and within the European Union (EU). The EU, comprising 28 countries prior to the June 2016 secession vote of the UK (still not fully implemented), had an estimated total of 1,078,900 Jews in 2019 (80.5% of the continent's total) (DellaPergola, 2020a).

The primary concern for Jews, as for many others, focused on the need for political and economic stability in Europe in general, and in the EU, in particular. Historically, Jews preferred to reside within multinational structures that were non-exclusive and multicultural. Jews – as any other sector of European society – shared and were bound to be affected by social changes – for better or worse. Since the dissolution of the Soviet Union, the European Union has constituted the main area of residence, hence an influential frame of reference for Jews in Europe. Under these circumstances, the nature and the quality of interaction between Jewish minorities and national majorities within European societies becomes important. The crucial issue is whether or not a tolerant and pluralistic environment can be created across the European continent, within the EU and outside it, where various national and religious cultures can be recognized as equally legitimate and where minority cultures which are not defined by a specific territory can obtain the same recognition and legitimacy as territorially based majorities (DellaPergola and Staetsky, 2020).

According to Webber (1994), Europe's Jews are both "a series of locally defined peoples" and "a single people with a common destiny, common identity and sense of purpose." (p. 6). Jews perceive themselves as part of a Jewish collective and, at the same time, as being part of a series of independent nation states. Thus, whilst possibly claiming a common Jewish identity, they must simultaneously define themselves contextually, be it in France, where the concept of a Jewish people is 'unconstitutional,' or in Belgium where *Shechita* (animal slaughter according to Jewish dietary laws) was outlawed in 2017 in the south Belgian region of Wallonia.

The concept of Jewish Peoplehood is one of the stronger unifying features of Jewish identity in Europe, with 90% saying it is important (68% claiming it is 'Very important') to their Jewish identity. Each Jewish community must confront its own national situation on the unique terms presented to it. The fact that Jewish schooling is free in Britain is of no relevance to Jewish education in France. That *Shechita* is proscribed in Sweden does not impact the availability of *Kosher* (following Jewish dietary law) meat in Italy. Yet Jewish education is no less important to French Jews and *kashrut* is no less important to Swedish Jews (Graham, 2018).

Thus, Jewish identity and identification in Europe are not homogeneous but rather complex and influenced by the country in which Jews live. A recent survey published by Graham (2018) regarding Jewish identity and identification among Jews who reside in eight European nations (France, Belgium, UK, Italy, Germany, Hungary, Latvia and Sweden) reports on Jewish identity as more heterogeneous than homogeneous. Unlike the world's two largest Jewish populations, Israel and the United States, Europe's Jewish population is scattered across various nation states. The few common components of Jewish identity emerging from the report are a strong sense of importance attached to remembering the Holocaust and a feeling of being part of the Jewish people. Supporting the state of Israel is also an important component in their ethnic identity and is expressed by frequent visits to Israel, among other activities.

Local culture in each country has a significant impact on the construction of ethnic identity, as do local policy toward ethnic minorities and the size of the local Jewish community, which makes it possible (or not) to provide religious services, including Jewish day schools. Regarding Jewish practices, only 30% of European Jews preserve the laws of *Kashrut* (regulations of Jewish dietary laws) in their homes, and this differs according to country of residence as well as socioeconomic status (Graham, 2018).

Among the Jews of Europe, observance of religious commandments and signs of Jewish identification have been on decline since the 1970s. After the Cold War, Western European Jewry diminished demographically and many Jews assimilated. Ties to the Jewish community weakened and many Jews abandoned most religious commandments with the exception of circumcision and burial customs. Synagogue attendance began to wane, as did observation of the *Kosher* dietary laws and of other Jewish commandments. The State of Israel became an important source of identification for Jews in many communities in Europe, and support for Israel increased. Since 1967 this support for Israel has turned into a civil religion of sorts. Nonetheless, in the wake of the wave of terrorism that washed across Europe in the 1970s and the 1980s, Israel became a burden and a source of suspicion and fear in the lives of European Jewish communities, due to the link between Israel and the Jews. One manifestation of this was the increase in terrorist acts specifically targeting European Jews. Jewish institutions of all types were forced to redouble their security measures. The attitude toward Israel became hostile. Anti-Zionist Jews called for a reexamination of their relations with Judaism, Jews and the Jewish people. In this atmosphere the question of Israel's place in the life of the Jewish community was repeatedly raised (Wasserstein, 1996).

Recently, studies indicate that Europe's Jewish communities are changing in their structure. A high rate of intermarriage in the second half of the 20th century was seen initially as a threat. Children with one Jewish and one non-Jewish parent tend to be identified as Jews than in the past. In addition, younger Jews are intermarrying less often than their parents did (DellaPergola and Staetsky, 2020; Echikson, 2021).

Jewish Europe can be seen as divided into two blocks with regard to ethnic identity and identification. In most of West Europe (eight countries, including France and Belgium), very strong attachment to the EU is a minority sentiment: 8%-21% of Jews feel this way. Furthermore, in that respect, attachment of Jews to the EU in West European countries is only very slightly higher than is the case among the national populations. The situation is different in East Europe (Hungary and Poland), where about one half of Jews feel very strongly attached to the EU versus less than 20% in the respective national populations. In the modern period, Jews were mostly recognized as a distinct religious group vis-a-vis the majority's society. The typically representative institutions of the Jewish community were those of a religious group. The alternative possibility of a definition along ethno-national criteria was not conceivable in the ethnocentric and quite monolithic cultural framework which prevailed in most Western national states. In the French tradition, which was to exert significant influence throughout the continent, Jews were indeed granted equal civil rights as individuals, not as a corporate group (DellaPergola and Staetsky, 2020).

Jewish-Israeli immigrants constitute part of the Jewish communities in West Europe. According to the latest available data from European statistical authorities, close to 70,000 people born in Israel reside permanently in Europe. In the current study Israeli emigrants constitute a significant part of the participants, particularly in Brussels and Antwerp (for elaboration regarding this population, see Chapter 2). Thus, in the following paragraphs I will describe briefly previous findings regarding their ethnic identity and affiliation with Jewish communities and Israel.

Israelis identify themselves mostly as secular and their main ethnic identity is Israeli; they hardly integrate with local Jewish communities (Dimentstein and Kaplan, 2017). A comparative analysis among Israelis who had defined themselves as 'secular' prior to migrating to cities such as Paris, London, Sydney, Los Angeles and New York, in the course of their lives in the Diaspora felt the need to become involved in Jewish communities in order to reinforce their Jewish and Israeli identity. First-generation migrants felt that their Israeli identity was central to their identity as migrants. They reported on this identity in terms of their military service, the climate in Israel, speaking Hebrew, ceremonies and rituals, shared history and food. The advantages of the cities to which they moved included primarily the possibility of good employment and high quality of life. While their Israeli identity was familiar and central to them, their Jewish identity was acquired during their time spent abroad (Gold, 2002).

Rebhun (2014) conducted a study comparing Israelis living in the United States to those in Europe in the context of cultural patterns and transnationalism. General findings showed that social integration, amount of time in the migration destination and civil status act together to reinforce ethno-religious identification. Various measures of assimilation into the host society serve to place obstacles in the way of affinity to the homeland, while ethno-religious culture is not a significant factor in transnational identity and identification with the homeland. Transnational ties and identity turn into identification with and ties to the Diaspora, the longer Israelis live in the destination country. Israelis living in the United States identify more with Judaism, engage in Jewish ceremonies and feel connected to the local Jewish community, while those living in Europe reported having mostly Israeli friends, an affinity for Israeli culture and more frequent visits to Israel (Rebhun, 2014).

In another study (Lev Ari, 2013) Israeli immigrants in London and Paris perceived their Israeli national identity as central to their ethnic identity as migrants and represented themselves as Israelis on many opportunities. In London,

Israelis over the age of 35 preserved their Israeli identity. They expose their children to other Israelis and thus prevent total assimilation. Israelis over-35 in London have a stronger Jewish identity than do young Israelis under the age of 35. Young, under 35 Israelis, mainly those in Paris, have few opportunities or little desire to preserve their Israeli identity. Some of the young people living in Europe make friends with non-Jewish local young people (Lev Ari, 2013). Rebhun and Pupko (2010) found that Israelis living in France identify themselves more as Jews than do those living in Britain when it comes to fasting on *Yom Kippur* (the Day of Atonement), observing the dietary laws and celebrating the Passover *Seder* (Yearly Passover night family gathering, commemorating the exodus from Egypt). In both of these countries, France and Britain, half of the respondents sent their children to Jewish schools of one sort or another, full time or part time.

This monography mainly focusses on analyzing and explaining patterns of socio-cultural integration, acculturation as well as ethnic identity and identification of two groups of Jews: Native-born and immigrants, residing in three cities, Paris, Brussels and Antwerp. By using qualitative and quantitative data, I will first describe respondents' socio-demographic and socio-economic characteristics. Then, I will analyze patterns of their inter-relations and integration among native-born non-Jewish majority, attempting to determine if they assimilate or segregate from the majority; I will also examine their perceptions regarding antisemitism. Another component, on the descriptive level, will focus on respondents' assimilation and acculturation strategies (Berry, 2001; Berry, 2005): Do they tend toward integration, separation, life within an environmental bubble, assimilation or marginality? How are respondents' social networks structured? Are they transnational, diasporic or local and non-Jewish? Ethnic identity and identification reported by respondents will be also significant components of the findings: Identity and identification with migrants from the same country of origin in the city of residence – diasporic; b) Identity and identification that cross national borders – transnational and c) General-civic non-Jewish identity – segregating versus assimilative.

The empirical basis for this study includes data collected via closed-ended questionnaires (455) and semi-structured interviews (22) which were conducted during 2017, in the three cities. The questionnaires, as well as the interviews, were conducted in Hebrew, English or French.

The quantitative method will provide a descriptive analysis of independent and dependent variables including means, standard deviations and frequencies. Inferential statistics will be used here to compare between native-born and immigrants, as well as by city of residence, based on correlations, t-test, ANOVA and multiple regression analysis.

The qualitative method was based on face-to-face semi-structured interviews which were conducted primarily by me, while among French speaking participants I was accompanied by local research assistants for translation. Interviews were transcribed verbatim, and content was analyzed by grouping main themes into common topics that were meaningful for the research questions (Creswell, 2014). Respondents were selected using purposive non-probability convenience 'snow-ball' sampling. No statistical probability sampling was carried out, since there were no data available for the Jewish population as such. Data regarding the size of Jewish populations in Europe and their socio-economic characteristics are available in most countries of Europe except for France and Belgium, due to these countries policy towards minorities (see Staetsky and DellaPergola, 2019). Thus, the claim to represent the entire Jewish population living in Paris, Brussels and Antwerp is impossible. Furthermore, the number of respondents from Paris is 247 (54%), 151 from Brussels (33%) and 57 from Antwerp (13%); thus, Brussels is over-represented while Antwerp is under-represented. The snow-ball sampling ended in over-representation in Brussels, while the under representativeness of Antwerp also results from the fact that more than half of the Jewish community there is ultra-Orthodox; they are reluctant to participate in any survey (see also Ben-Rafael, 2017). Nevertheless, the high number of respondents (455), as well as the use of mixed methods, makes it possible to learn about the characteristics, perceptions and feelings of Jews residing in these cities. In addition, I will compare some of my findings to previous studies for further validation.

In the course of the research, I received assistance in contacting the research population from the Israel Ministry of Absorption and from its representative organization (The Israeli House) in Paris, as well as from local Jewish organizations. About six local research assistants distributed the questionnaires to their Jewish relatives, friends and people in their social networks.

1.7 Structure of the Book

This book is organized around eight main chapters; each includes a concise summary and discussion of its main findings. The first chapter introduces foregoing review of theoretical literature regarding social migration, ethnic identity, socio-cultural integration and acculturation of migrants and ethnic minorities, followed by a review on world-wide Jewry as privileged minorities versus antisemitism, with special focus on Jews in contemporary Europe. Chapter 2 describes the study participants: Characteristics of their socio-demographic, socio-economic and Jewish-background. Based on quantitative data, I will describe the participants' profile by three cities of residence and between native-born and immigrants.

Chapter 3 centers upon participants' macro perceptions, regarding non-Jewish communities in their cities of residence. They were asked to describe the various populations in their city of residence and the dynamics of their structure, focusing on native-born versus new waves of immigrants, both Jewish and non-Jewish. In this chapter I base my analysis on qualitative data, since the questions in the semi-structured interviews were aimed to provide more comprehensive information regarding perceptions of inter-relations between ethnic groups in each city on the macro level, and the dynamics characterizing them in the last few decades.

Chapter 4 presents participants' perceptions and attitudes regarding their personal economic, professional, and socio-cultural integration into the majority. I use quantitative and qualitative analysis in order to describe patterns of integration into the majority society in each city, and compare between native-born and immigrants. This chapter also describes predispositions towards emigration which reflect on various components of participants' integration.

Chapter 5 focuses on contemporary antisemitism, as perceived on the macro level, and, particularly, as personally experienced by interviewees. This chapter is based mainly on qualitative data regarding antisemitism and includes a short quantitative paragraph, which describes respondents' attitudes towards possible future emigration because of antisemitism in each city, and between native-born and immigrants. Chapter 6 turns to in-group perspectives, namely participants' macro and micro perceptions regarding ethno-demographic, denominative, and organizational changes in local Jewish communities as well as their own involvement in them. I base my analysis on qualitative and quantitative data, which provide a dynamic profile of these communities, their contemporary structure and vitality, as well as personal experience and involvement in the structure of local Jewish communities and their social networks.

Ethnic identity and identification will be the focus of Chapter 7. This chapter will present both quantitative and qualitative analyses which point out differences in patterns of ethnic identity and identification among participants, comparing between three cities, as well as between immigrants and native-born. The concluding discussion in Chapter 8 links general theoretical concepts with empirical findings regarding two Jewish communities in three cities and the challenges of integration, acculturation and identity. It commences with patterns of integration, segregation and assimilation into the non-Jewish majority, followed by the Jewish communities themselves: Their characteristics of continuity and vitality, and cultural integration within Jewish communities, namely ethnic identity and acculturation. The chapter concludes with suggestions for policy trajectories and possible future research regarding Jewish communities in contemporary Europe.

Chapter 2
The Participants: Socio-Demographic and Socio-Economic Characteristics

2.1 Overview

This chapter will introduce the participants: Their socio-demographic and socio-economic characteristics. Based on quantitative data, I will describe the participants' profile by three cities of residence, and between native-born and immigrants. These two comparisons are particularly important since data regarding the size of Jewish populations in Europe and their socio-economic characteristics is available in most European countries except France and Belgium. This is due to the fact that in the two countries Jews cannot be identified as a religious group (as is the case in the United Kingdom) or as an ethnic group. The official French census, by law, does not record religious affiliation. Thus, in France there are other data sources such as national surveys, Jewish communal registers and surveys of the local Jewish community, while in Belgium there are only Jewish data sources (Cohen E. H., 2009; Staetsky and DellaPergola, 2019). Therefore, estimations of the Jewish population might vary from one source to another and sometimes lack recent socio-economic data.

Jewish-Israeli immigrants constitute part of the Jewish communities in West Europe. According to the latest available data from European statistical authorities, close to 70,000 people born in Israel reside permanently in Europe. Over 60% of Jewish Israelis who were born in Israel, reside in the four largest Jewish communities of Europe: The UK (about 18,000), Germany (10,000), France (9,000), and the Netherlands (6,000) (DellaPergola and Staetsky, 2020). Most Israelis live close to Jewish communities, mainly in the large cities (Rebhun and Lev Ari, 2010). Migration from Israel is voluntary and the pull factors attracting migrants to the destination countries are much more dominant than the push factors motivating them to leave Israel. Indeed, Israeli migrants can be seen as the 'product' of global trends of economic integration alongside the weakening of nationalist-Zionist ideology that used to attribute major importance to settling in Israel (Lev Ari and Cohen N., 2012).

Since most Jewish immigrants to France and Belgium constitute less than a third of the Jewish population in the broader framework of Jewish immigration to Europe, Israel was one of the prominent suppliers of more recent immigrants (see also DellaPergola and Staetsky, 2020) who participate in my study, particularly in Belgium. Therefore, I will present findings from

https://doi.org/10.1515/9783110698817-002

previous studies regarding this specific group of new immigrants in this and other chapters.

France has the largest Jewish community in Europe. Core estimate for French Jewry decreased to 450,000- the third largest Jewish population in the world (DellaPergola, 2020a). France is known to have one of, if not the largest *Sephardi* community in the Diaspora. Jews of *Sephardi* ancestry, mostly first, second, or third generation immigrants from North Africa – the Maghreb (the first generation immigrants arrived between 1955–1965), clearly predominate numerically (75%) over those of Central-Eastern European origin who, until World War II, constituted the main component of Jewish population (DellaPergola, 2017; DellaPergola, 2020a).

Most Maghreb Jews came from Algeria (130.000). Following the new political and social order, as well as the Israeli Arab conflict after 1948 and its effects on the rising of anti-Jewish hostility, Maghreb Jews decided, at that time, to emigrate from their countries of origin (Abitbol and Astro, 1994; DellaPergola, 2011b). Others emigrated from Tunisia (50,000) and Morocco (30.000) (Bensimon and DellaPergola, 1984). Accordingly, most Jews living in Paris are *Sephardi* Jews. A minority are *Ashkenazi* Jews of European origin. The median age of Jews in France is 55 years (Graham, 2018). Among Israelis living in France, 6,600 are native-born Israelis and another 10,000 were born elsewhere and immigrated first to Israel and then to France. Israelis constitute two to three percent of the Jewish population of France (Cohen Y., 2011; DellaPergola, 2017; Rebhun and Pupko, 2010). Today, about a third (34%) of Jews in France are immigrants, versus only 12% among the total French population (Graham, 2018). Currently, more than half of the Jews live in the greater Paris metropolitan region (Cohen E. H. and Ifergan, 2003; Fourquet, 2015). Jews who reside in Paris are more integrated in the wider society compared with those in other areas in France. They also have much higher education – at least a bachelor's degree: 73%, compared to 66% of other Jews in France, and 50% among the non-Jewish population in the country (Cohen E. H., 2009).

The social and economic mobility of the second generation of East European immigrants, the influx of North Africans, and the gradual implementation of the urban renewal program caused a considerable change in the once Jewish districts and affected the dispersal of Jews throughout other districts of Paris. The greatest change took place in the neighborhoods that in 1956–1957 were still inhabited by artisans and small traders of East European origin. By 1968, the residents of these neighborhoods had been replaced by the most impoverished of the North African immigrants. Between 1945 and 1968, the urbanization of the Paris region became accelerated. In 1941, 10% of Paris Jews resided in the inner suburbs of the city; by 1966 about 20% were living outside the city limits. North African Jews were partly relocated in the large housing developments reserved for repatriated citizens. Between 1957 and 1966, the number of Jewish communities in the Paris region rose from 44 to 148. Like other suburban inhabitants, Jews were employed mostly in Paris (Jewish Virtual Library, 2021).

The Jewish population in Belgium was estimated at 29,000, in 2019, which makes it the world's sixteenth largest Jewish community (DellaPergola, 2020a; DellaPergola and Staetsky, 2020). Most members of the Belgian Jewish community today were born in Belgium (Ben-Rafael, 2017). According to Graham (2018), 27% of the Jews in Belgium are immigrants, compared with 16% among the total Belgian population. Half of the Jews in Belgium live in Brussels, the French-speaking capital, and the other half in Antwerp – the northern, Flemish-speaking part of Belgium (Ben-Rafael, 2017).

As mentioned earlier (Staetsky and DellaPergola, 2019), the Belgian Jewish population is among the least documented in Europe. In absence of a census or a central Jewish community register, directories of Jewish organizations or commercial activities aimed at a Jewish public provided a useful, though rough proxy. The relatively stable numbers are due to a higher rate of natural increase among the traditional Orthodox community in Antwerp and the growth of a large European administrative center in Brussels that attract Jews from other countries (Ben-Rafael, 2017; DellaPergola, 2017).

Most members of the Belgian Jewish community (74%) today are *Ashkenazi* Jews born in Belgium, the descendants of former immigrants from East and Central Europe before World War II and Holocaust survivors. Jews from North Africa came to Belgium in small numbers during the 1960s, after the French decolonization (Ben-Rafael, 2017). Another study, based on a sample of 786 Jews (FRA, 2019) presents somewhat different data: 64% are native-born and 78% consider themselves *Ashkenazi* Jews. The median age of Belgian Jews is relatively young (compared with that of French Jews) and equals 52.5 years (Graham, 2018). In the absence of broader and more representative data, my current study compares data with some socio-demographic and socio-economic data of a study based on 438 Belgian Jews respondents (Ben-Rafael, 2017). The rate of married Jews in Belgium is 66% and 73% had at least some kind of post-secondary education – academic or professional. Most respondents were employed: Among them 36% were salaried employees and 27% self-employed. The vast majority belongs to the middle class, whose main occupations used to be in textile and leather goods (Ben-Rafael, 2017), which are probably different now (as I will demonstrate in my findings). According to figures based on Cohen Y. (2011), there are 2281 Israelis in the country.

In the next section I will describe in detail findings from the current study regarding socio-demographic characteristics of Jews by their city of residence. Albeit recent, most of these findings are absent from contemporary studies, particularly in France and Belgium. Thus, some of them will be compared with previous studies while others are specific to this study.

2.2 Socio-Demographic Characteristics by City of Residence

Participants (455) in this study reside in two countries, France (55%) and Belgium (45%). Most Jews, world-wide, reside in cities (Rebhun and Lev Ari, 2010; DellaPergola 2017); thus, I decided to focus on those residing Paris, Brussels and Antwerp. The actual number of Jewish communities in these cities was 275,000 in 2019; whereas more than half of French Jews reside in Paris, in the Belgian cities around 15,000 live in each city (DellaPergola, 2020a). The participants of the current study reside in Paris (54%), Brussels (33%) and Antwerp (13%). Obviously, there is over-representation in Brussels, due to the sampling method bias, and under-representation in Antwerp, as a result of the large portion of the ultra-Orthodox community, which is usually reluctant to participate in surveys (see also the methodology section).

Another major comparative component in the current study is place of birth: Either native-born (Europe) or immigrants. More than a half of the respondents (58%) are native-born, while the rest are immigrants (42%). Among those who reside in Paris the majority are native-born, and about a third are immigrants (similarly to Graham, 2018), while in the Belgian cities the rates of immigrants are much higher than what was found in another study, particularly in Antwerp. The total average rate of immigrants in the two Belgian cities is 51% (in both cities the number of immigrants is 107, divided by total sample 208), which is significantly higher than the rate of 36% immigrants among 786 Jewish Belgian respondents of the FRA survey (2019), but similar to the average percentage of all immigrants in Brussels, which equals 62% (IOM, 2015), and that of Antwerp, which is 42% (Saeys et al., 2014).

Most immigrants (71%) are long-term immigrants (see Chapter 1 for elaboration regarding the term 'dichotomy'). Paris has the highest rate of long-term immigrants, while in Brussels the rate of short-term immigrants is the highest (Table 1).

Table 1: Countries of origin by city of residence (percentages).

Countries of origin/city	Paris	Brussels	Antwerp	All	Difference Sig.
Total	100	100	100	100	**
Native-born (France/Belgium)	65	54	33	58	
Foreign-born (immigrants)	35	46	67	42	
Countries of birth	100	100	100	100	**
Europe	66	72	52	66	
North Africa	24	6	2	15	
Israel	6	19	38	14	
Other countries	4	3	8	5	
Term since immigration	100	100	100	100	**
Long-term immigrants (15 years or more)	86	54	68	71	**
Long-term immigrants (14 years or less)	14	46	32	29	

*.05 or less; **.01 or less.

Women, who responded to a higher degree than men (although not signi-ficantly) were in their forties; among them, women from Antwerp are the old-est. Compared with Graham's (2018) findings, the average age of both French and Belgian Jews is higher (in their fifties) compared with this study. While Parisian Jews and those from Brussels are similar in their family status (about two thirds are married), almost all from Antwerp are married. Compared with Ben-Rafael's study (2017) the rate of married participants is higher in this study's average of the two Belgian cities (66 and 77, respectively), primarily due to participants from Antwerp. Although most participants are citizens, those from Paris have higher rates of citizenship compared with the two Bel-gian cities, who have more participants of other civil status. This results from the fact that in the Belgian cities there are more immigrants primarily Israelis (Table 2).

Although respondents come from various neighborhoods (particularly in Paris – about 50), some neighborhoods have more Jewish residents than others. In Paris, the following quarters (arrondissements) are the most prevalent: The 17th (19%), the 19th (14%), the 20th (12%), the 16th (9%), the 12th (8%) and the 11th (5%). There are other areas in greater Paris, as well as the center, such as the 13th quarter, or *Colombes à Fontenay-sous-Bois*, which populate one to four percent of Jewish residents, each. When asked about the 'Jewishness' of the neighborhood,

Table 2: Socio-demographic characteristics by city of residence (percentages and means).

Socio-demographic characteristics/city	Paris	Brussels	Antwerp	All	Difference Sig.
Gender (female)	58	61	67	60	n.s
Age in years (standard deviation)	44 (16 years)	42 (14 years)	48 (12 years)	44 (15 years)	*
Family status	100	100	100	100	**
Married or permanent spouse	66	59	95	67	
Never married	19	29	0	20	
Divorced	10	9	3	9	
Other	5	3	2	6	
Civil status	100	100	100	100	*
Citizens	83	71	71	77	
Permanent resident	12	22	20	17	
Temporary resident	4	5	9	5	
Other	1	2	0	1	

*.05 or less; **.01 or less; n.s.= not significant

81% of respondents reported that it has primarily Jewish character, such as the following quarters: The 19th, the 11th, the 16th, and the 12th. The city's most famous old Jewish quarter, since the Middle Ages, the Marais, in the 4th arrondissement (see also Laguerre, 2008) was not represented at all in this study, probably since most Jews in Paris reside in other neighborhoods. In Chapter 3 of this manuscript some interviewees refer to specific neighborhoods, such as the 16th and 11th quarters with regard to their Jewish residents.

In Brussels, out of 27 different neighborhoods, the most prevalent are Uccle (43%), Rhode Saint-Genèse (12%), Forest (9%), Ixelles (7%) and Anderlecht (6%). In rest of the neighborhoods the percentage is of one to two. Most respondents (84%) reported that neighborhoods are Jewish in character, particularly Uccle, Ixelles, RhodeSaint-Genèse and Forest.

Finally, in Antwerp, seven neighborhoods were reported by the participants. The most prevalent neighborhoods are Antwerp center (50%), where most Jews reside, Edegem (20%), Wilrijk (18%) and Berchem (8%), where more non-Orthodox and richer Jews live (see also Gsir, 2016). The other two were reported by two percent each. Indeed, participants residing in the so-called

'Jewish neighborhood,' which is located partly in the somewhat impoverished area around the Central Station and in an adjacent historically bour-
geois borough are over-represented. The Jewish neighborhood is known for
its very visible strictly Orthodox and Hasidic Jewish population, whose presence in Antwerp is historically related to diamond trade and industry. The
neighborhood's population also consists of white non-Jewish Flemings and,
since the 1990s, immigrants from East Europe, India and other countries
(Vollebergh, 2016). Going back to this study's results, surprisingly, only 70%
described their neighborhood as having Jewish character, primarily those residing in Antwerp center, Wilrijk and Edegem. Probably the last two and
other prevalent neighborhoods have a large portion of non-Jewish residents
and Jews who reside there are less religious and of higher socio-economic
status.

2.3 Socio-Economic Characteristics by City of Residence

As for their socio-economic characteristics, almost two thirds of the participants have higher education, mostly graduates. However, as Table 3 indicates, participants from Antwerp have the lowest higher education, while
those from Brussels have the highest rate of undergraduates and graduates. Parisians are characterized by having participants from both ends of
the distribution: Either ones who have academic degrees (55%). or those
with non-academic degrees (45%). Cohen E. H. (2009) addressed the Parisians' relatively high socio-economic status, but his study was conducted 18
years ago.

There are numerous occupations participants mentioned in the questionnaires (more than 50, which were recoded to 10). There are differences when
compared by cities. Brussels and Paris have the highest percentages of free professionals, which is correlated to the higher educational attainments in these cities. Paris and Antwerp have relatively many teachers. Brussels has the highest
student rate, probably due to this city's younger age, as well as governmental
employees and clerks. Antwerp has the highest rate of housewives and unemployed, maybe since part of the respondents are ultra-Orthodox women with low
rates of higher education. Finally, the rate of retired participants is much higher
in Paris and Antwerp than in Brussels, which reflects age differences (although
the Parisians are not the oldest, a fifth of them are retired). More than half of the
participants are salaried workers, particularly in Paris, which might explain their
higher rates of retirement. Another explanation lays in the retirement policy
in France; full-benefits retirement age is 62 (Nossiter, 2020) compared with the

age of 65 in Belgium (Chini, 2019). While the vast majority in both Belgian cities own dwellings, less than half of the Parisians own apartments or houses. This finding is similar to general data regarding dwelling ownership among French people (ESREA France, 2016). As for Antwerp, it seems that the sample in this study, with regard to dwelling ownership is similar to that of a survey which indicates that in relation to people who rent, the majority are private tenants (Gsir, 2016).

Table 3: Socio-economic status by city of residence (percentages).

Socio-economic Characteristics/city	Paris	Brussels	Antwerp	All	Difference Sig.
Education	100	100	100	100	**
Elementary/high school	30	15	19	23	
Non-academic education	15	14	31	17	
Under-graduate	11	23	33	18	
Graduate/Ph.D.	44	48	17	42	
Occupation	100	100	100	100	**
Free profession	20	24	8	20	
Teachers	16	7	16	13	
Managers	7	13	13	10	
Non-academic occupations	5	2	0	4	
Students	5	19	0	10	
Sales/business	12	10	11	11	
Blue-collar	8	2	11	6	
Public/governmental workers	5	17	14	10	
Unemployed/housewives	1	1	14	2	
Retired	21	5	13	14	
Occupational status	100	100	100	100	**
Salaried	65	51	35	56	
Self-employed	23	31	37	28	
Non-employed	12	18	28	14	
Dwelling ownership (yes)	43	78	83	60	**

*.05 or less; **.01 or less

In the last decade there is significant emigration, particularly from France to Israel and other destinations (DellaPergola, 2020a). It is possible that a large portion of these emigrants have high socio-economic status, since for these immigrants it is easier to leave and find better opportunities elsewhere (see also Rebhun and Lev Ari, 2010). However, the general profile is that Parisians' socio-economic status is rather high, although there is a portion of middle-lower class. Regarding those from the Belgian cities there is only general reference by Ben-Rafael (2017) to their successful economic integration in Belgian society, which is true mainly of Brussels residents.

A single interviewee (A. from Brussels) shed light on contemporary young Belgian Jews, who unlike their parents (see also Ben-Rafael, 2017), have higher education and more opportunities to integrate in numerous occupations:

> I would say the majority from Brussels are locally born and bred. They are working in all kinds of occupations, there's not one specific occupation. There used to be one specific occupation in Brussels for Jews, which was called the *Shmates* [miscellaneous used clothing]; it's the textile, well, clothing. And now it's finished. The new generations are channeled to all kinds of occupations, usually fairly higher level in society business, independent people, lawyers, doctors, etc. I would say the vast majority of Jews in Brussels are those people.

In my study, Antwerp participants have the lowest socio-economic status, regarding higher education attainment and occupational prestige, although they have the highest dwelling ownership.

2.4 A Comparison between Native-Born and Immigrants according to Background Characteristics

When comparing between native-born (58%) and immigrants (42%), there are some characteristics which are similar, such as gender and dwelling ownership: 60% are women in each group and 60% own dwelling. Significant differences were found in their socio-demographic characteristics regarding age, familial status and country of birth. Native-born are younger (40-year-old and standard deviation=14 years) than immigrants (50 years old and standard deviation=15 years). Accordingly, there are more participants who have never married (28%) among the native-born, compared with only 10% among immigrants, while 64% are married in the first group and 72% in the other (the rest have other familial status such as divorced).

Another important difference is between participants' and their parents' countries of birth. Naturally, almost all native-born (98%) reported that they were born in Europe. The rest (2%) also arrived as very young children, between the ages of one to three and thus are considered native-born or second generation immigrants (see Lev Ari, 2012). Among the immigrants 35% were born in North Africa, a third in Israel, 23% in Europe (countries other than France or Belgium) and 9% in other countries. Similarly, native-born parents were mainly from Europe (half) and North Africa (more than a third), while immigrants' parents were born in North Africa (40%), Europe (a third) and Israel (16%). However, despite the differences in countries of origin, the participants define their ethnic attachment in a similar manner: About half as *Sephardi*, forty percent as *Ashkenazi* and the rest – as 'other' (less than 10% in each group).

As for socio-economic status, native-born have higher educational attainments, whereas 47% have advanced degrees (Masters and Ph.D.) compared to 36% among the immigrants. The most common occupations among participants (more than 50 types of occupations mentioned by respondents) in the two groups are professional, free occupations; medical doctors, lawyers and engineers, among others, are more prevalent among native-born than among immigrants (14%). Another profession which was common is teaching (15% among native-born and 11% among immigrants). The rate of students among native-born is almost twice as high as among immigrants (11% and 7%, respectively). Other occupations which were found to be different are business and sales (14% among native-born and 7% among immigrants), clerks and government (15% among immigrants; 6% among native-born). The rate of retired people is much higher among the immigrants: Twenty seven percent versus only six percent among native-born. As for their occupational status, there is no significant difference between the two groups: About 55% are salaried and a quarter are self-employed. The rate of unemployment is slightly higher among the immigrants compared with native-born (19% and 14%, respectively). Thus, it seems that in most components, the socio-economic status of the immigrants is lower than that of native-born. Naturally, civic status is also different when the two groups are compared: While almost all native-born (89%) have citizenship and the rest are permanent residents, only 62% of immigrants have citizenship and 28% are permanent residents (the rest have other temporary status).

2.5 Summary

Paris is the demographic center of Jews in France and more than half of them reside there. In this study the sample includes Jews from numerous neighborhoods in greater Paris and almost all its quarters; it provides a diverse and maybe representative picture of Jews from different backgrounds. Brussels and

Antwerp are the two main cities where the vast majority of Belgian Jews reside. Although the distribution is based in this study, some characteristics still resemble previous studies' findings, while others are new.

With all limitations, there are some findings which seem to indicate new socio-demographic and socio-economic characteristics. Similarly to another study, Jews in Paris are mostly native-born, and a third are immigrants, whereas those in Belgian cities have a higher proportion of immigrants than what was reported in a previous study regarding Jews in Belgium, particularly regarding the rate of Israeli immigrants. Thus, the current study can elaborate knowledge on Israeli immigrants in these cities on the one hand, and present Brussels and Antwerp as more diverse with regard to their local Jewish community's character and its constant change due to the arrival of new immigrants. The younger ages, particularly among those from Brussels, also indicate the demographic vitality potential of the Jewish community, which is partially explained here by the large section of new immigrants. Furthermore, relying on one interview, it seems that while the old generation worked in textile business, the younger generation has higher socio-economic status and chooses diverse occupations.

As anticipated, in line with previous studies which refer to Jewish communities in general in France and Belgium, countries of origin differ also among the three cities: Whereas most of those in Paris have North African parents, those from the Belgian cities have mainly European roots. Ethnic origin affiliation as *Ashkenazi* or *Sephardi* are unique to this study, since this component of self-identification according to city of residence was not studied before, and it is highly correlated with parents' countries of origin. Three quarters of those who reside in Paris define themselves as *Sephardi* while the same percentage of Jews residing in the Belgian cities consider themselves *Ashkenazi*.

Each city has its own socio-economic profile, according to educational attainment, occupational prestige, dwelling ownership and rates of employment. In Paris and particularly in Brussels the socio-economic status is high with regard to respondents' higher education attainments and occupational prestige. However, the Parisians have dual socio-economic status, which can be partially explained by high rate of emigration among those who have more income and educational attainment. These findings are more detailed, unique and new compared with other previous studies. The Antwerp sample has much lower socio-economic status, probably due to the ultra-Orthodox portion characterized by low educational attainments and higher rates of unemployment (which also result from their relatively older age). The surprising finding is dwelling ownership: Although a large portion of Parisians have high socio-economic status they have lesser ownerships percentages compared with those in the Belgian cities, particularly in Antwerp. This can be explained by the fact that until 2015 many rich French Jews bought houses and apartments outside of France, in Israel for example, and some of them emigrated as well. In addition, since this pattern of residence ownership is similar to that of the general population in France, apparently it is part of a cultural norm and not of low socio-economic status. The more affluent may prefer to spend their money on vacations and leisure activities. Finally, this study supplies detailed data regarding neighborhoods of residence in each city. While most of those from Paris and Brussels report on residing in what have recently become Jewish neighborhoods, usually characterized by the residents' more prestigious status, those from Antwerp still mostly reside in what is known as typical Jewish neighborhoods. The ultra-Orthodox Jews in Antwerp tend to stay in the center of the city, while others, probably secular Jews, find other and more prestigious neighborhoods. In both cases, the neighborhoods are more ethnically diverse than those in Paris and Brussels.

When compared by two groups – native-born and immigrants – the differences are less significant than by city of residence. The most striking finding in this regard is in the socio-economic status; though, similarly to migration theories, some migrants experience upward mobility in the country of destination, there is a gap between them and the local native-born. Since the immigrants in this study are older and most of them arrived decades ago (particularly in Paris), it seems that the gap might not be ignored. Generally speaking, immigrants with higher socio-economic status experience better opportunities for upward mobility and in a short period. However, for those who arrive with lesser educational attainment and fewer economic resources, it takes many years, and sometimes the gap between them and the native-born is maintained for several generations. Since most immigrants in the Belgian cities are relatively new comers, with higher socio-economic status – as other studies imply- this group of immigrants might obtain higher status and become similar to native-born, unlike those in Paris.

Chapter 3
Inter-Relations between Jewish and Non-Jewish Communities in Paris, Brussels and Antwerp: Macro Perceptions

3.1 Overview

This chapter will center upon participants' macro perceptions, regarding non-Jewish communities in their cities of residence, populations that characterize them and the dynamics of their structure, focusing on native-born versus new waves of immigrants. In this chapter I will base my analysis on qualitative data, since the questions in the semi-structured interviews were aimed to provide more comprehensive information regarding perceptions of inter-relations among ethnic groups in each city on the macro level, and the dynamics characterizing them in the last few decades.

I will begin by a general introduction regarding recent social urban policy trajectories towards immigrants and minorities in both France and Belgium (for earlier integration policies see Chapter 1). The overview will be followed by two 'findings' sections, which will focus on participants' perceptions regarding city and neighborhoods' changing ethnic structure, followed by their descriptions of inter-relations of ethnic groups in their city of residence. A short summary will conclude this chapter.

Paris is a 'world city,' namely, the place where the agglomeration of demand by multinational headquarters meets the agglomeration of supply by advanced producer services (APS) firms. This is also referred to as 'intensive globalization' (Robinson et al., 2016). Paris is one of today's global cities characterized by dynamic and intensive social change, political conflict and cultural innovation and gulfs based on exclusion and inclusion. Immigrants and ethnic groups might belong to those who are included, but still, most of them, particularly immigrants suffer from some degree of exclusion (Castles et al., 2014).

Social policy towards immigrants and minorities in France which was aimed to eliminate the poor neighborhoods of migrants (*bidonvilles*) in Paris and other large cities in the late sixties, made public housing more accessible to these immigrants and tried to create housing dispersal to improve their assimilation in the cities. By the 1980s, social policies focused on urban youth and improved housing, social conditions and education among migrants. The effects of these policies are minor and until today a large portion of these migrants and their descendants are excluded and segregated. These exclusion

https://doi.org/10.1515/9783110698817-003

patterns were manifested in 2005 by violent riots of Maghreb and Turkish youth of migrant background. However, some migrants have integrated into the host society and experienced upward mobility and are part of the dominant culture. These migrants are less segregated as an ethnic group and some are almost totally assimilated (Castles et al., 2014).

Furthermore, various aspects of French urban policy regarding ethnic neighborhoods have emphasized the notion of social and ethnic balance to prevent the spatial concentration of immigrants, the ghettoization of their residential space and the polarization of ethnic communities, as well as to enhance their incremental integration in daily French life. The French municipal government sees ethnic enclaves as impeding assimilation and as potential sources of conflict. Therefore, the municipality views the role of the state as upholding the common good in its planning policy above the ethnic good (Laguerre, 2008).

Immigration to Brussels began relatively late, in the 1980s, but due to the large number of immigrants an immigration policy was needed already in the early years. As early as 1981, immigrants in Brussels accounted for 24% of the total population; some came to work in the many international institutions in the city (Adam, 2013). In the past, a policy of national integration was introduced in Brussels, and ethnic and cultural diversity was not taken into account, but today, Brussels is an ethnically and liberally diverse international and multicultural cosmopolitan city. The immigrant population in Brussels is very active, and has representation in local politics. However, the government tackles a high unemployment rate; it opens schools to provide equal opportunity, provides vocational courses for students dropping out of schools and encourages the employment of people at low socioeconomic levels, including immigrants (Deveeshouwer et al., 2015).

Today, Brussels is a world city that combines different and diverse ethnic and cultural groups. As the center of the European Union, Brussels has a special status attracting many immigrants around the various EU institutions, such as the European Commission, lobby offices and EU embassies (Favell et al., 2007). Brussels-Capital is the region where the greatest number of foreigners live, proportionately to the population. The share of foreign-born residents in Brussels is 62% (IOM, 2015).

Furthermore, the region constitutes the main gateway for international migration, as approximately 11% of its active population are recent immigrants, i.e. of foreign nationality and who have lived in Belgium for less than five years. Thus, the integration of new immigrants in the host society has been a challenge for the city authorities for many years. Special programs are intended for migrants and offer them (or require them to take) language, citizenship and shared values courses or professional training. Recently, the refugee crisis in Europe, and especially in its capital, as well as the question of their integration in society in the coming years, have made matters worse for these institutional and political policy makers. There is still lack of understanding and some dissension coming from both sides (Xhardez, 2016).

A study conducted by the International Labor Office in Belgium (BIT[2]) regarding the employment rates of work-migrants in Brussels found that there is discrimination against them, even at the stage of applying for work, which is one of the reasons for the high number of unemployed immigrants. In 1998, with the support of European bodies, anti-discrimination activities began, mainly in the field of private employment (Tandé, 2015).

Nevertheless, Brussels offers a relatively high access to 'quality of life' benefits particularly for skilled migrants, compared to other so-called 'open' and 'global' cities such as Amsterdam and Paris. This openness is due to the exceptional combination of its cosmopolitan, multicultural bi-national nature, European role and deregulated markets. Furthermore, there is the presence of many young Europeans, mainly of the Flemish, who are open to the cultural, political and social ideas and are considered more open to change and innovation. Not only is Brussels portrayed as a global city in terms of social and political networks, but it also has a history of rare ethnic, cultural and religious diversity in Europe due to the many ethnic groups living in the city. It is a unique multicultural capital city located at the crossroads of French, Flemish, German and English. It is influenced by each of the languages but is not unambiguously defined by any of them. This is an example of a capital city that is not influenced or controlled by one national society, and its immigrants experience more *'Europeanness'* than any other capital city in Europe; as a result, it offers a particularly interesting field of research (Favell, 2001).

Antwerp is the largest city of the Flemish region in Belgium (Saeys et al., 2014). Antwerp's history of migration reflects Belgian migration history; however, it also has some specific features of its own, mainly due to the presence of the harbor and the activities related to it. As the first migrants were recruited in the coalmining industry, they arrived mainly in Wallonia where the coalfields were situated. As soon as the Belgian state allowed migrants to work in other sectors like industry and services, migrants from other countries such as Greece and Spain, and later from Morocco and Turkey, dispersed in all the other major Belgian cities – including Brussels, but also in Flemish cities such as Antwerp with its port or Ghent in eastern Flanders. After the EU enlargement of 1985, migrant workers from Portugal also arrived in Antwerp, although a larger proportion of them went to Brussels (Gsir, 2016). With its international seaport,

---

2 Bureau International du Travail.

Antwerp has been attracting immigrants from distant places for a long time. While Antwerp has a population of more than 500,000 residents, it has been estimated that 42.1% of its inhabitants are of foreign descent (Saeys et al., 2014).

Experience in Austria, the Netherlands and Belgium is similar: While national-level politicians rejected long-term integration, city authorities recognized diversity in urban populations and provided services to minorities, including welfare, health and education. Current migration to Europe since 2000 increased significantly, channeling migrants to various western countries such as the UK, France, Belgium and the Scandinavian countries. However, France is the only major immigration country where immigration has stagnated beyond the 2000s. Asylum seekers are the most recent immigrants to Europe, France and Belgium, included. Thus, migration to Europe since 1945 has led to growing cultural diversity and the formation of new ethnic groups. Part of them are visible through their looks, language and neighborhoods, as well as ethnic organizations (Castles et al., 2014).

In light of the above description of relatively liberal attitudes towards formal social integration of immigrants and minorities in France and in Belgium, I will present the state of research regarding current manifestations of the opposite end-rising antisemitism towards Jews in these countries.

As residents of these cities in France and Belgium, Jews constitute part of the urban fabric; to most cities Jews immigrated many years ago, during the fifties through the seventies, or they are native-born. Newly arrived immigrants reside mainly in the two Belgian cities. Thus, in all three cities the Jewish communities are well established, although they have been undergoing changes, on which I will elaborate in the next section, and discuss through qualitative analysis, to be presented later in this chapter.

3.2 City and Neighborhoods' Changing Ethnic Structure: "Where Jews Arrive the Prices Go Up"

As a rabbi, M., a long-term immigrant from Israel, describes the social structure of Paris neighborhoods from a macro level.[3] He focuses on Jews versus Muslims regarding their behavior in the neighborhoods and particularly praises positive integration within Jews:

> The 16th quarter is extremely wealthy [. . .] where Jews arrive the prices rise. Before they arrived, it was possible to buy an apartment there, now it is impossible. On the other

---

3 The quote in the title is from an interview with Rabbi M. from Paris.

hand, where our 'cousins' [an Israeli nickname for Muslims, L. L.] live, the prices drop and you can see garbage in the streets. It is hard to recognize the place. If you look at photos made 30 or 40 years ago, it looked like France. When Jews arrived, they brought some culture [. . .] ethics [. . .] they behaved like French people.

S., who immigrated to France in his teens, also described Paris neighborhoods where most Jews currently reside: "Now there are more Jews in the 17th quarter in Boulon. Jews constitute 12,000 out of 120,000 residents. I think that in the 16th quarter there are at least twenty synagogues. The population there is very strong, the 16th quarter is the 'golden triangle' of Paris."

When I asked D., a long-term immigrant from Israel to Paris, to elaborate regarding his neighborhood (the 11th quarter), he described it as one that went through gentrification recently: "Today its name is *Oberkampf*, after the main road [. . .] which became very trendy. Until two decades ago it was a commercial street where nothing happened at night, everything was dark [. . .]. Today everyone wants to live here, it has every potential for prosperity." D. describes in detail the development of the neighborhood where he resides and the gentrification process there: "At the beginning students arrived here since rental rates were low, and then all these people who came to eat couscous and buy special Moroccan shoes [. . .]. Finally, more well-off families and guys who had more money [. . .]. That is why this neighborhood turned into a sort of 'bubble.'" D. describes this neighborhood as once, some decades ago, being composed of immigrants from North Africa and Africa, and as still having a mosque of radical Muslims. I asked D. to elaborate on the mosque; he claimed that while being a hipster neighborhood it is characterized by going through contradictory processes of secularization on the one hand, and the rise of the local mosque which is particularly important to new immigrants, on the other:

I lived in front of this mosque in 1984 [. . .]. In the last few years there is rise in the Islamic faith and the mosque is quite full [. . .]. Since there is not enough room inside the mosque, they pray on the side walk in two parallel very long lines. Some are not from the neighborhood; they come from far away, Chechens, Afghans and Syrians.

R., a native-born, resides in another Parisian neighborhood, which he describes as Catholic, 'typically French,' that is, ethnically quite homogenous. His children, when they were young had mostly French friends at school. However, he is aware that, as a result of immigration from Africa, France in general is more diverse these days. "There are ethnical groups. Like everywhere in France, a lot of different people, but not too many, concentrated in this area. When our kids went to school, the majority of kids were born here, and most of them from French parents. [. . .] But this area here, is really typically French, I would say. Many people are Catholic."

S. describes the changes in Paris, in the last thirty years through the skin color of the residents which became much darker: "In the past the vast majority in Paris were white [. . .] they did all the hard work. But they were French and white [. . .]. For twenty to thirty years there was immigration and the quarters changed. North and east Paris became darker and more Arabic."

In Brussels, according to Rabbi A. (an immigrant *Habad* emissary. *Habad* is a Hasidic movement) the complex of immigrants is different than that described by interviewees in Paris; there are North Africans but mainly Turks, who have an impact on the city: "[Immigrants] came from North Africa, Turkish communities [. . .] they make big presence in Brussels, in politics; they are often in the news."

A., also a Brussels resident, native-born, gave a very good description of the various groups who reside in Belgium in general and in Brussels – in particular. He refers specifically to new immigrants, Muslims, the European Union and NATO employees and immigrants from Kongo. Regarding new immigrants, A. describes their impact on the city. He compares new to old immigrants, and emphasizes that the first group is much more visible in the infra-structure of the city, politically and economically:

> There is of course a lot of immigration, still today. So that changes the face of the city very much. There are still first [generation immigrants] coming in, but second and third generation, who in the past used to be very quiet, you didn't hear from them, and they would not dare to speak out. It's totally changed now: They have gained empowerment, more strength and I think pride. This means that they are much more visible in all types of activities, outside, in economic and political life, in local activities. It's a big change in Brussels, especially in some neighborhoods.

A. also refers to other groups of immigrants who reside in Brussels – the European Union employees. Apparently, he appreciates these groups more than those he previously described, regarding their socio-economic status, their European culture, knowledge of languages and positive contribution to the city:

> In addition, you have a totally different population. I guess they don't mix. As I mentioned, [they] work for the EU and NATO, etc., are usually highly educated and very highly paid people, speaking many languages, having many degrees, often from different countries, mixed marriages, from France, Finland, Italy, Holland, etc. and this is really where you see Europe.

Another group of immigrants that A. describes, came from Congo, a former Belgian colony. This community is also described by him in a positive manner, both concerning their characteristics and positive integration, compared to the new Muslim immigrants to Belgium:

And there has always been in a nice, I think, very colorful and happy African community from Congo. You know, Belgium used to have Belgian Congo until 1960 [. . .] it was called Zaire before, now Congo again; they came to live here and they're usually very well integrated, probably better than the Muslims, I think.

M., also a native-born from Brussels refers to the changes that occurred in the city, particularly in the make-up of pupils in public schools and Muslim dominance, compared with the Christian, regarding the food pupils are asked to bring along according to Muslim laws [*Halal*]: "Nowadays in the state schools, they even sometime ask the Christian not to bring sandwiches with pork. Sometimes the Muslim ask to have *Halal* food provided by the school. In our time I would not even dare ask someone to change his/her habits."

In sum, interviewees in Paris and in Brussels referred to the various ethnic groups in their cities from different angles. Some pointed to the Jewish and non-Jewish composition of the neighborhoods, particularly in Paris. The Parisian interviewees described the socio-ethnic structure mostly by pointing to changes by quarters. They emphasize the positive integration of Jews as residents, and their contribution to the development of the neighborhood and thus, to its high prestige. On the other hand, new Muslim immigrants and black people from Africa are perceived as damaging the neighborhoods and impact their deterioration. Other interviewees gave a more general description of the ethnic changes in the neighborhoods, as part of gentrification. In Brussels, the comparison was made among different groups of immigrants, and not by neighborhoods; whereas those employed by EU organizations seemed to be more favorable and alike Belgian culture, new Muslim immigrants were perceived as dominant in various areas and not in a positive manner. Antwerp interviewees did not relate to these macro components; their words will be presented in later sections.

3.3 Inter-relations among Ethnic Groups in City of Residence: "It Feels Less Secure Outside"

An interesting and complex picture emerges from the interviews when interviewees are asked about the relationship between various ethnic and immigrant groups in the three cities, Rabbi M. described generally good inter-relations with the local majority, Christians, both Catholic and Protestant, who constitute, according to his estimate, about 60% of Paris population, as well as with moderate Muslims:

> With the Cardinal of Paris, Andre Van Trois, a great person, there are good connections. With Protestants as well. We also have good relations with a very moderate mosque, existing here in Paris for 70 years, La Mosquée de Paris. But these Muslims do not represent the 'real Islam' in France; they are here to calm things down.[4]

D. described France and its attitude towards its foreigners as of very delicate interactions, based on the republic's three main values of 'liberty, equality and fraternity' (*Liberté, Égalité, Fraternité*) on the one hand, while being cautious towards strangers since World War II, on the other. D. was concerned by the last terror attacks and even stated that they intimidated the 'bubble' he and his neighborhood residents had lived in:

> As a result of World War II trauma, when French people cooperated with the Nazi regime, [the attitude towards minorities] probably disturbs French people's collective conscience. Thus, many people are reluctant to say things that are not politically correct [. . .]. After the last terror attacks, there is tremendous anxiety, no one knows which direction this society is heading to [. . .]. They know that some people who live here despise this society and its values [. . .]. It creates a schizophrenic and very uncomfortable situation which explains the rise of the far right, of which the bubble I live in is very afraid.

S., who immigrated to France from Morocco almost four decades ago, describes excellent integration of Jews in France, so that besides their Jewish family names they are totally French:

> Generally speaking, the Jewish population in France is well integrated into the French social fabric. [. . .] In culture, in commerce and in finance. They are integrated on all levels. [. . .] There are names of those who feel they are not originally French, Jewish names, names from North Africa [. . .] that can express that they were immigrants. In Paris you don't feel it anymore, because most Parisians are immigrants.

However, there is a slight contradiction between the harmonious perception of integration of French Jews within the majority and S.'s recognition of security or safety issues:

> Jews are integrated on all levels, in all professions. Maybe even in the most prestigious professions. It is impossible to say that there is any racism towards them. [. . .] But on a daily basis, it is impossible to say that Jews feel deprived at some point. They enjoy everything every Frenchman enjoys. [. . .] Apart from the security part that bothers them, it is impossible to say that Jews suffer more from racism. Certainly not like Arabs, nor like Negroes.

S. perceives new immigrants as threatening, compared to the past, whereas he himself feels safe. He demonstrates this through a personal story:

---

4 The quote in the title is from an interview with S. from Paris.

. . . A feeling, I don't know if it's true, but it feels less secure outside. I remember that as a pupil I came back from Morocco, visiting my parents [. . .], the aircraft arrived late at night to Paris [. . .] I took a train and then I arrived to a close train station for my connection – it was midnight. I remember that as a 16 year old child, I slept with homeless people outside. They brought me some cardboards to sleep on. I kind of worried since I never slept outside at night and I slept with them. In the morning they brought some milk and gave everyone, they got milk and croissants somewhere. It felt safe. So, the population has changed.

H., an Israeli long-term immigrant to Paris, elaborates on the negative cultural changes in the city, as a result of the arrival of new immigrants. She particularly refers to the dirt and their customs which are not appropriate to the local European-French culture: ". . . So it became stinky here and I have a feeling of third-world [. . .] streets which are more appropriate to Brazil than to Europe. The French people are very quiet, they are afraid to respond [. . .]. It is forbidden to talk since you might be considered 'racist', and these days it is like a curse."

In a similar manner, Rabbi M. describes new Muslim immigrants' integration as problematic. He seems to criticize the way they are using welfare policy in France:

There is a very good thing here in France. Apartments that belong to the state [. . .]. Very nice apartments, very well kept by the state. They are constantly renovated and well maintained. Look at pictures of these apartments forty, fifty years ago. They were nice. See how they look now, like trash cans. Sometimes the state has to give them an alternative hotel for three or four months to renovate the apartments and bring them back. But two or three years later it looks as if the building went through a world war.

Rabbi M. seems to be bitter regarding welfare payments and rights the new Muslim immigrants obtain from the country: "For every child they receive three hundred euros. If they arrive with three, ten children, it's three thousand euros, in addition to what the mother and father are entitled to since they do not work. Five thousand euros, and the apartment, education everything is for free."

On the other hand, Rabbi M. praises the Jewish immigrants who came from the Maghreb countries to France and Israel in the sixties. While those who arrived to France experienced positive upward mobility and integrated into French society, those who came (from Morocco) to Israel experienced the opposite:

[Jews] came from various places. They became more French than French native-born [. . .]. Among the Jews who arrived from North Africa to this country, you can find many medical doctors, senior engineers. They are tremendously successful, in comparison to those who arrived to Israel and became blue-collar workers.

R., who also resides in Paris describes the second-generation Muslim immigrants as having split identity which makes them feel alienated from French society: "Today, the second generation, is a little angry, because they feel that they are not French completely, and they are not any more Arab either. And so, they, many of them have difficulties in finding their place."

J., a long-term immigrant from England, who resides in Antwerp describes the immigrant population as diverse and mainly living near the central station but not in her neighborhood. They consist primarily of Turkish immigrants, but also of other Muslim immigrants who immigrated recently and who make her uncomfortable, since they keep their tradition to a larger extent than several years ago:

> So, like I said, you are here, this is a very Flemish or white area, but you'll go five minutes from here and it will be a completely Turkish area. And those areas are sometimes like you have in Brussels, they can certainly be a discomfort [. . .]. You never used to have that twenty years ago. All the girls covering themselves, they never did that. It's something quite new.

In addition, J. describes inter-relations between the local, native-born residents and immigrants in her neighborhood. One Turkish family resides in her street and according to J., every one acts in a polite manner towards them but locals do not invite them to their homes. She thinks that this so called nice and polite attitude towards the immigrants is insincere: "That family comes and everybody shakes hands and this is the only Turkish family in the street, but nobody would ever invite them over [. . .]. Do people really feel close to the immigrant here? No. It's nice, it's phony nice."

Rabbi A. describes the relationship between immigrants, ethnic groups and native-born as apparently friendly. However, when it comes to real relations of friendship, the native-born are reluctant to create social ties. He specifically mentions their avoidance of saying good morning in the street, which makes him feel a stranger: "Everybody is very friendly to everyone, but the depth of friendship is questionable. Here, once you have a friend he is loyal, but at the beginning everybody is almost afraid to say good morning to others in the street or to the neighbors, so I do feel a bit outsider, but in time you melt in."

In addition, Rabbi A. refers to the Syrian refugees in Brussels. He and his community organized some events for the refugees' children, in order become closer to them. This was also an act of solidarity with groups of foreigners in the city and part of the collective memory of being Jewish refugees in the past:

> There are Syrians, and we for example, visited their school [. . .] in a refugee camp [. . .]. We joined a campaign, called 'love the stranger' because we were once foreigners as well, so we were also refugees. [. . .] We collected many things, especially school equipment, and we sat with them. It was a very nice and inspiring experience.

A., who was born in Belgium and resides in Brussels, presents a more complex picture regarding inter- relations between native-born and new immigrants. He claims that native-born are disappointed with these immigrants. A. makes distinctions between the various immigrant groups. He perceives those who come from East Europe as industrious and harmless, as well as striving to achieve upward mobility. On the other hand, the Muslim immigrants do not integrate in the city and are responsible for the violent incidents in the city:

> I think many people had hoped it would work well, and it didn't work that well [. . .], [they are,] very disappointed I believe. [. . .] I'm not talking about the EU type of people, because they are fine, I would say. I'm not talking about the East European because they work very hard, but they don't make much trouble. They drink a bit too much, maybe. They don't really make much trouble, and they try to push their children usually for a better life, get up a bit on the social ladder. The Muslims [. . .] don't make enough effort to integrate, to participate. And now after all this violence, disappointment turns a bit towards anything.

Jewish interviewees describe good relationship between native-born and immigrants, Christians, Muslims and Jews, who have been living in the country for some decades, primarily Jews. They seem to perceive both Jews and Muslims who arrived during the fifties to the seventies as having common culture, values and norms. However, when it comes to their attitude towards new immigrants, the interviewees seem to be xenophobic and even racist towards the newcomers by associating them with insecurity, terrorism and exploitation of the welfare system and public property-in the three cities. Thus, while Christian East European new immigrants are more welcome, Muslims are perceived as challenging European culture in various ways, both in France and Belgium.

A. also comments on changes which occurred in Europe regarding policies of multiculturalism. Until recently, most European countries promoted multiculturalism with regard to religious and cultural practices; lately, there is a demand from foreigners to integrate in the cultural infrastructure, to leave their bubble, including Jews. He demonstrates this policy change through the Jewish custom of animal slaughter [*Shechita*]:

> I believe that up to now it was a big thing in Europe, to keep, to preserve and permit the religious communities to live exactly like they wanted, to give them freedom, including total freedom in terms of *Shechita*, for example . . . There is a trend now-more and more people say you should integrate and you should not have special treatment and they believe that *Shechita* is anachronistic as a system and it harms the animals . . . Not only does it harm the animals, but on top of it, it keeps you in your little bubble and we don't want that.

When I asked the following hypothetical question: "If someday all Jews residing in the city left, what would happen?" few answered this question.

Rabbi Y., who arrived to France from Morocco in his youth, decades ago, replied that it would be a severe loss to the city, in view of Jews' significant contribution: "I think if all the Jews of France left France, France would become a country similar to those in Africa, where there is nothing. Today look at France: Who are the greatest in every area? [..] Look how many Jews there are, [. . .] doctors, lawyers, etc."

R., a native-born from Paris, notes that emigration of all Parisian Jews would undermine French culture in general and the identity of France, in particular: "If 300,000 Jews from Paris emigrate [..], it will undermine French culture. I think France will lose some of its identity by losing half of French Jews."

Y., an immigrant from Israel who was born in Libya and currently resides in Antwerp also thinks that if Jews left the city, it might be problematic, as they are professionals who contribute to the development of the city: "Like my children who gained diplomas, occupy many offices. Antwerp will be very sad if the Jews leave. It will be a huge loss."

Compared to the interviewees from Paris and Antwerp, A., a resident of Brussels, does not believe that the influence of Jews in his city is significant. Although there are lawyers and doctors and other professionals who provide services to the city residents, the cumulative impact of the Jewish community is not great at all: "Not so much, I think. As I feel, there's a lot activity in the professions, you know, lawyers, doctors, [. . .] it's more general service to the population I would say, it's not much of an impact [. . .]. If they were all to leave tomorrow, it wouldn't change, not at all."

3.4 Summary

When asked to describe inter-relations and patterns of integration of the various ethnic and immigrant groups, most interviewees who elaborate on this issue, seem to feel that immigrants from earlier waves (fifties to seventies), Jews in particular but even Muslims, integrated well within the Christian majority in Paris, both culturally and socially.

However, when it comes to new Muslim immigrants, interviewees express entirely different feelings, including fear, strong resentment, unease and even disgust. One of them even refers to second-generation Muslim immigrants who still have not integrated, have split ethnic identity and are alienated from the host society. Some interviewees supplied another macro perspective to recent majority-minority relations, claiming that the French republic seems to be very cautious, as a result of World War II, to manifest any racist acts, despite the recent terror attacks, and thus it enables the far right to rise, and take more decisive acts against new immigrants.

Interviewees in Antwerp describe similar feelings of unease towards new Muslim immigrants, who are perceived as religiously more extreme than those who arrived in earlier decades. When it comes to local neighborhood relations, interactions between immigrants and locals are discreet but there are no real social connections. In Brussels, interviewees' attitudes and feelings seem similar to those voiced by the Parisians, but since there are also groups from East Europe, it is obvious that the last group is more appreciated and accepted compared with new Muslim immigrants who are perceived as a 'disappointment' by the locals. Only one interviewee, who is a rabbi, expressed some compassion towards Syrian children refugees and organized some help for them.

New Muslim immigrants are definitely more present and higher in number in Paris, and thus attract most interviewees' (mostly negative) attention. In Antwerp and in Brussels there are other new immigrants who come from more similar cultures (for example, those who work in EU offices) or from higher socio-economic status and are therefore described as less intimidating and more favorable, although not entirely welcome by the Belgian host society. Still, particularly those from Paris, perceive the impact of the Jewish community in France in general, and in Paris in particular, as still very significant with regard to economic and cultural life.

Chapter 4
Between Integration within the Non-Jewish Majority and Segregation

4.1 Overview

This chapter focuses on economic, professional and socio-cultural integration of respondents. I used quantitative and qualitative analysis in order to describe patterns of integration within the majority society in each city and country, and between native-born and immigrants. In the last section I describe predispositions towards emigration which reflect on various components of participants' integration.

As mentioned in Chapter 1, there is a problem in achieving socio-demographic data regarding Jews in France and Belgium, since the law does not permit the identification of a religious or ethnic group, unlike the case in other European countries. Thus, in France there are other data sources such as national surveys, Jewish communal registers and surveys of local Jewish communities, while in Belgium there are only Jewish data sources (Cohen E. H., 2009; Staetsky and DellaPergola, 2019). In this manuscript I elaborate not only on socio-demographic characteristics of Jews in these two countries, but also add a quantitative and qualitative analysis of various components of their integration.

The chapter opens with an overview which describes patterns of integration among Jews in France and Belgium, primarily after World War II. The 'findings' section will commence with a general, quantitative, descriptive analysis of all interviewees' perceptions regarding the various aspects of their integration within the majority, to be followed by two sections which present qualitative data regarding patterns of professional and socio-cultural integration versus segregation in each city, and between native-born and immigrants. Finally, a quantitative paragraph, followed by a qualitative one, will focus on respondents' attitudes and motives towards possible future emigration. Different motives for emigration can serve as possible indicators for successful integration, versus segregation (see also Lev Ari, 2015) among both native-born, old and new immigrants in each city of residence. A summary will conclude this chapter.

Jewish presence in France dates from the early Middle Ages. During the medieval period France was widely known for the quality of its *Torah* (the substance of Jewish teaching) scholars. As a result of the French Revolution in 1789, France became the first European nation to emancipate its Jews, although antisemitism persisted for centuries. When analyzing by ethnic origin, *Sephardi*

https://doi.org/10.1515/9783110698817-004

immigrants who came to France in the 1950s and 1960s are somewhat less integrated than *Ashkenazi*, who have been in France for several generations. Thus, *Sephardi* Jews have somewhat lower levels of education and income. However, compared with other migrant populations in France, Jews from North Africa are well integrated and assimilated into French society (Cohen E. H., 2009). Furthermore, compared with previous Jewish immigration from Eastern Europe to France (after World War II), those who came from North Africa were acquainted with the French socio-cultural structure and could better integrate in the host society. North African Jews who arrived in France in the seventies enjoyed an era of individualism and upward mobility that characterized French society at that time. Since then, Jews in France have been taking part in economic prosperity, political stability and have been living among Catholics who accepted Jews (Cohen M., 2000). Later on, Jewish immigrants from North Africa to France (during the fifties through the seventies) were more successful in integrating in French society than were other immigrants to France (Cohen E. H., 2009; Everett, 2017).

Today, there is relatively high representation of French Jews in academic, executive, managerial and liberal professions (physicians, dentists, medical experts and advocates). Over the last quarter of the 20th century there has been a change in patterns of employment types: The percentage of French Jews who are workers or merchants has steadily dropped, while employment as senior executives or as those who pursue liberal and academic professions has grown (Cohen E. H., 2009).

Paris is the center of intellectual and cultural life of French Jewry. In 582, the date of the first documented evidence of presence of Jews in Paris, there was already a community owning at least a synagogue. After World War II, Paris and its suburbs contained about 60% of the Jewish population of France. Between 1945 and 1950 the Jewish population of the area grew from 125,000 to 150,000, and in 1968 it was estimated between 300,000 and 350,000 (about 5% of the total population). In 1950 two-thirds of the Jews were concentrated in about a dozen of the poorer or commercial districts in the east of the city. Jews constitute a sizable minority in Paris itself (about 6% – 8% of the total population) and in several suburban towns.

The large wave of immigration of Jews originating from North Africa in 1955–65 changed the ethnic composition of the Jewish community in the Paris area: *Sephardi* Jews are now the majority, even if, with the exception of Alsace, *Ashkenazi* Jews outnumber the *Sephardi* in other regions of France. Within Paris itself, the formerly typically Jewish neighborhoods have taken on *Sephardi* features. Some are on the way to disappear, while others have been 'Judaized.' Parisian Jews who live in every district in the city. The Jewish population of the Paris region is very mobile, partly due to constant urban renewal. In their new places of residence, they establish new communities, most often with *Sephardi* majority. Jews are represented in every type of occupation and practice in all professions. They play an important role in Parisian academic circles (Jewish Virtual Library, 2021).

New Jewish immigrants to Europe arrive from Israel (for more elaboration see Chapter 2). A study conducted among Israelis who live in 27 European countries, characterizes them as engaging mainly with Hebrew-speaking and Israeli networks, both online and by face-to-face interactions. They are also moderately engaged in local Jewish communities for specific events and services but not as active members of these communities (Dimentstein and Kaplan, 2017). Another study comparing Israelis residing in Paris and in London (Lev Ari, 2013) found that Israelis in London were more connected to the organized Jewish community than were Israelis in France.

Jews arrived in the Netherlands from the 13th century, after their exile from England and France. In 1831, when Belgium gained its independence, it acknowledged Judaism as one of the religions in the country. Judaism during this period became a personal and private matter, and the only public expression of religion was governmental recognition of community leaders. Furthermore, Belgian constitution emphasizes several amendments (*La Constitution Belge*, 2019, see, for example, Articles 10–12; 19–20) regarding minorities' rights for equal status, freedom of religion and ceremonies which also attracted Jews – both secular and religious (World Jewish Congress, 2020).

In the 19th century, Brussels became the main Jewish center in Belgium, but with rising waves of immigration from Eastern Europe, Jews moved to Antwerp, where the Jewish community grew significantly from the beginning of the 20th century. The rise of Nazism in Germany led to the immigration of some 25,000 German and Austrian Jews to Belgium. In the late 1930s, almost 95% of Belgian Jews were immigrants (Schreiber, 2000). After World War II, many Jews returned to their original homeland, without family and friends, and were forced to re-establish their communities. This time immigration to Belgium was almost completely halted, except for a few thousands from Egypt and the Maghreb countries (Ben-Rafael, 2017; Schreiber, 2000).

Antwerp has attracted a significant portion of Jews for centuries, a characteristic which is typical of its municipal migration history. After Belgium's independence in 1830, Jewish migrants arrived from central and Eastern Europe and their community developed progressively. Before World War II, more than half of the 100,000 Jews in Belgium lived in the city. Nowadays, the Orthodox Jewish community of Antwerp is one of the largest in Europe, comprising about 15,000 persons (Gsir, 2016). Antwerp is also internationally known for its diamond trade, a sector that has been dominated by the large Orthodox Jewish community in the city, although recently Indian dealers have become more prominent in it.

(Saeys et al., 2014). The Jews of Belgium are socially and economically assimilated into Belgian society and are no longer considered immigrants. The vast majority of Belgian Jews belong to the middle class and work in the textile and leather industries in Brussels, and in diamonds and commerce in Antwerp (Ben-Rafael, 2017).

4.2 Integration within Non-Jewish Majority Communities: Social, Communal and Cultural

Quantitative data, collected from respondents' questionnaires reveal that integration within the non-Jewish majority is quite moderate. The most prevalent components of integration are economic relations: Consumer services and business matters. All other components of integration, social, cultural and communal, range between low to medium extent. Marital ties and common children's education are low as well. Respondents' answers are extremely heterogeneous (high standard deviations). The highest homogeneity emerges in responses regarding contributions to non-Jewish institutions, which indicates that not only is it rare among respondents, but also typical of most of them (Table 4).

A comparison between native-born Jews and immigrants indicates three significant differences. While contributions to non-Jewish institutions in city of residence are generally infrequent, they are more prevalent among the native-born group than among immigrants (mean=1.97; standard deviation=1.17 and 1.70; 0.96 accordingly). Moreover, as of spending leisure activities together, again, native-born reported higher rates, compared with immigrants: (mean=2.46, standard deviation=1.25 and 2.15; 1.15, respectively). Finally, native-born reported higher rates of intermarriage with local non-Jews (mean=2.34, standard deviation=1.31) compared with immigrants (mean=2.03; standard deviation=1.27).

With respect to respondents' integration into the three non-Jewish communities, significant differences emerged in all components. Respondents from Brussels scored highest on close social relations with non-Jewish residents, although their average relations with non-Jewish residents are only moderate. Both Antwerp and Paris scored similarly low on close social relations with non-Jews. Regarding close economic ties with non-Jews, again Brussels is highest and differs from Paris, while Antwerp resembles both; it is between Paris and Brussels. With respect to cultural and leisure activities with non-Jews, again Brussels is the highest, differing from the other two cities, which resemble each other on this variable. Intermarriage with the non-Jewish community is infrequent among all respondents, though such marriages are more frequent in Brussels than in the other two cities, where such marriages are rare, particularly in Antwerp. Joint education with non-Jewish children, mutual assistance, contributions to non-Jewish institutions and activities as a cohesive community are more prevalent in Brussels and less in the other two cities. Finally, usage of non-Jewish services is the most prevalent component among respondents in general; Antwerp residents are the most active in this area (Table 4).

Table 4: Integration components with local non-Jewish community, as perceived by respondents – by city of residence. ANOVA (1= Not at all; 5= To a very large extent).

	All (N=440)	Paris (N=242)	Brussels (N=143)	Antwerp (N=55)	Significance of differences
	Mean (SD)	Mean (SD)	Mean (SD)	Mean (SD)	
Strong social relations	2.75 (1.12)	2.52[1] (1.10)	3.24[2] (1.02)	2.52[1] (1.01)	F=.22.01**
Strong economic relations	3.07 (1.20)	2.81[1] (1.24)	3.46[2] (1.04)	3.11[1,2] (1.12)	F=13.63**
Mutual cultural activities	2.44 (1.21)	2.02[1] (1.11)	3.13[2] (1.12)	2.40[1,3] (1.04)	F=44.42**
Mutual leisure activities	2.34 (1.22)	2.07[1] (1.18)	2.97[2] (1.13)	2.06[1,3] (1.03)	F=25.91**
Marital relations	2.22 (1.30)	2.04[1] (1.26)	2.83[2] (1.27)	1.52[3] (0.91)	F=22.56**
Joint children's education	2.14 (1.28)	1.88[1] (1.20)	2.63[2] (1.28)	1.96[1,3] (1.31)	F=16.19**
Mutual aid	2.48 (1.11)	2.27[1] (1.08)	2.90[2] (1.07)	2.28[1,3] (1.02)	F=16.19**
Donation to non-Jewish organizations	1.86 (1.09)	1.49[1] (0.93)	2.40[2] (1.17)	2.00[3] (0.88)	F=35.72**
Use of non-Jewish services such as supermarkets, clinics	4.08 (1.12)	3.95[1] (1.18)	4.14[1,2] (1.03)	4.51[2] (0.94)	F=5.88**
Act as a cohesive community	2.09 (1.12)	1.91[1] (1.08)	2.47[2] (1.13)	1.92[1,3] (1.02)	F=12.12**
Index of integration within the non-Jewish community (Cronbach's alpha=0.90)	2.57 (0.85)	2.33[1] (0.81)	3.01[2] (0.79)	2.48[1,3] (0.70)	F=34.56**

*P<.05; **P<.01.

Other social and communal components included in the quantitative analysis, focused on social networks and ethnic composition of neighborhoods. With regard to close friends, only 15% wrote that most or all of them are non-Jews, while 18% wrote that they have no friends from this group. Most respondents reported having few or about half non-Jewish friends (42% and 26%, respectively). Those from Brussels have the largest number of close friends among non-Jews: Fifty-two percent reported having about half or more non-Jewish friends, compared with those from Paris (35%) and Antwerp (31%). No difference was found when native-born and immigrants were compared in this regard.

When asked about the structure of their neighborhood, about half of the participants reside – to large and very large extent – in local, non-Jewish areas. The rest (47%) wrote that their neighborhoods contain few or none of non-Jewish residents. This pattern of residence is more typical of those residing in the Belgian cities than in Paris: Two thirds (Brussels) and half (Antwerp) of respondents reside in non-Jewish neighborhoods, compared with 44% in Paris. This pattern of residence is similar when native-born and immigrants are compared.

When analyzing[5] the impact of more background variables, such as gender, age, and ethnic origin (*Sephardi* or *Ashkenazi*), the most influential variable is city of residence: Those from Belgian cities, particularly Brussels, and *Ashkenazi* are more integrated in the local non-Jewish community, compared with Parisians and *Sephardi*. In addition, native-born are more prone to assimilation among non-Jews, compared to immigrants.

4.3 Professional Integration within Host Societies: "I Am Grateful to France"

In this section I will present qualitative data regarding interviewees' perceptions and feelings, with focus on their professional integration.[6] Some feel that France or Belgium offered them good opportunities for upward mobility, while others express more reluctant feelings in this context.

---

5 Using multiple regression analysis, standardized coefficients (Betas).
6 The quote in the title is from an interview with Rabbi M. from Paris.

4.3.1 Paris

Rabbi M., an immigrant from Israel, seems to be most satisfied with regard to his occupation and, according to him, also mission – as a major rabbi in Paris. Although he left his profession in Israel to follow his wife to Paris, due to her career motives to study medicine, he gradually became a rabbi due to his involvement in the communities in which he lived and his religious background. Looking back – about fifteen years after immigration, he describes enthusiastically the role of a rabbi in France, compared to Israel, as challenging and including many areas:

> The role of a rabbi in Israel seems limited [. . .] and here the role of the rabbi is to understand everything. You talk about medicine, you talk politically, you talk about financial ethics, you talk about people's lives [. . .]. There is something very personal here, in the job, the mission is very interesting.

He further elaborates regarding the opportunities for upward mobility that France enabled him, which are more favorable than elsewhere:

> With time you realize that [. . .] you give something, but in return, this country offered you opportunities that might not have been offered in another country. In Israel [. . .] there are lots of people who are talented; however, no one tells you that you are exceptional. I thank God for coming here and being able to express my inner abilities [. . .]. I am very grateful to France.

R., a native-born of France, notes that as a teacher he feels satisfied: "I am a teacher at a school in the sixth district of Paris. I am very satisfied with my financial situation. I think I earn very nicely for the work I do." When asked if he could be more successful elsewhere, he replied that language could be an obstacle to pursuing a profession elsewhere: "Given my profile, in the work I do, I do not think I can succeed elsewhere for now, just because of language difficulties." His wife, N., also notes that she is satisfied with her job as an accountant, and believes that it will take too much effort to practice the profession elsewhere: "If I have to leave I think I will have to study again [. . .] since accounting is different in each country."

O., a native-born, retired doctor notes that although in other countries he might have earned more money, he does not regret staying in Paris and pursuing his profession: "We could have made more money in another country or in other places, [but we] never looked at the situation from negative point of view. I never thought that I could go away to earn more money somewhere else." His wife, I., a native-born, notes that she is satisfied with her job as a saleswoman, and that she has voluntarily chosen to be a housewife. Although she says this with a laugh, her words imply that she regrets being prevented from returning to work. However, in her case her disappointment from not pursuing a career is not directed to France:

> I was very happy in marketing. When the third child was born, I told O., that I wanted to spend some more time with my children, so I stopped my job for more than 10 years or even 12. It was very difficult to come back to work, when I wanted to come back, it was really important for me. But, finally, at the company, they told me 'you're too old' [laughing].

Compared to other interviewees from Paris, D., a long-term immigrant from Israel, feels much less satisfied with his occupation and professional mobility in France: "I feel that my skills are not fully utilized [. . .]. I delude myself that one day I will realize a certain percentage of my skills. [. . .] I constantly wish for it with optimism and that motivates me." To my question, if he had lived in another country he might have been more successful in realizing his skills, he replied: "I think if I had been in Tel Aviv I would have had more economic means to realize artistic projects for example, which I can't do here. But maybe I'm telling myself stories I do not know." Hence, D. feels a certain degree of disappointment in terms of his professional fulfillment and thinks he might have been more successful in Israel, while others describe professional success stories that became possible especially in France, or at least satisfaction with their opportunities for social mobility in the country.

4.3.2 Brussels and Antwerp

M., from Brussels, describes the advantage of Belgium as a welfare state, and thus seems to be content with working there: "The advantages of working here, generally are that you have got social security which is more advanced, that you are much more protected here than for instance, in the US."

A., another native-born, describes his profession as transnational, and as such, he can experience working in other countries. Nonetheless, A. does not refer to his satisfaction with his occupation, but since Brussels enables these transnational connections, he seems comfortable with his occupation: "So my prime work place always has been, and still is in Brussels, here, in Belgium. Quite an international outlook as work, but still located here."

B., an Israeli immigrant residing in Brussels, expresses high satisfaction with her integration as a local Hebrew teacher, and similarly to A., seems to be at ease with becoming transnational: "In teaching, I would integrate everywhere. Again, if the place is a nice place, a supportive place, nice people. Here the place is very nice, I really like the school."

In contrast, her husband T., who followed her to Brussels, left his occupation in Israel, following his wife's desire and dream to live in Brussels. Implicitly, he is not enthusiastic about his work as a volunteer in the youth movement (*Hashomer Hatzair,* a Jewish socialist youth movement): "I actually retired from the army twenty or so years ago. After that I worked for almost two years in a factory. I did not know what awaited me here at all. So very soon, after three months, I already started getting involved here with the *Hashomer* [the youth movement]." When I asked him if he would rather have an occupation elsewhere, he evaded and replied briefly: "I guess I would not be idle anywhere. Everywhere I would find what to do."

L., the only interviewee from Antwerp who refers to this aspect, was a school principal in Israel and continues in this position since his arrival to the city about a decade ago, notes that he experiences a sense of satisfaction with his work: "I am very satisfied, otherwise I would not stay here for so many years. Even those who employ me think I do a good job, so in the meantime it looks good."

4.4 Socio-Cultural Integration with Non-Jews: "I Probably Live in a Bubble"

This section will present qualitative findings which reflect participants' perceptions regarding their integration in their city of residence, as immigrants or native-born.[7]

The semi-structured interviews indicate that interviewees describe in detail patterns of integration similar to those found in the questionnaires. Some feel more integrated within the majority and some are more attached to their Jewish ethnic communities. There are differences according to city of residence, as well as between native-born and immigrants.

4.4.1 Paris

D., who resides in Paris, mentions the term 'bubble' as reflecting his feelings residing in a multi-cultured world city: "I probably live in a bubble in a city, which does not reflect the rest of the city or the country [. . .]. There are immigrants and people with accents from all over the world [. . .]. Most of the people

---

7 The quote in the title is from an interview with D. from Paris.

with whom I am in contact are French." D. emphasizes his all-French affiliation and admits that his neighborhood does not reflect the city or as mentioned in the previous quote – the whole country. He seems to feel comfortable in this bubble and describes himself and his interactions with various groups in his surrounding as someone who "gets by with everyone." D. makes distinctions between the various groups and points to the term 'community' as threatening the nation state. He also praises inter-cultural differences and is not afraid of Islam and what it represents, since it expands and challenges multiculturalism in Paris:

> There are cultures which I find more difficult to handle, but I can live with pluralism in this neighborhood. In France there is a trend of returning to past communalism [. . .], which threatens the republic. They wanted to create a model of a citizen who is free of religious chains and now new communities emerge which demand separation from the republic and at the same time – they wish to become French. I am not afraid of Islam [. . .]. I respect differences and they are positive social phenomena which make you think and test your attitudes towards the Other.

S., a long-term immigrant from Morocco, who does not feel immigrant any more, describes his relationship with the gentiles (*Goiem,* as he calls them), as good, although there is a difference between them regarding the socio-cultural component, particularly concerning holidays and the *Shabbat* (Saturday):

> Feeling immigrant does not exist anymore [. . .], however, if you keep *Kosher*, wear a *Kippah* [head cover observant Jews wear] or a hat, do not participate in events of gentiles such as Christmas, you feel that you are not part of the neighbors in your building. You say hello, you know them, you chat with them even in the elevator, but there is some difference [. . .], you feel different.

Only few describe their social networks as composed of some non-Jewish friends. The few who do are long-term immigrants; two out of three are secular Israelis. As of others, they mainly mention Jewish friends; they will be described in one of the following chapters.

Rabbi Y., a long-term immigrant from Morocco, describes social networks based mainly on professional connections (as a rabbi in the French army) and therefore comprised of Jews and non-Jews. He also believes that mixed networks may be positively portrayed by gentiles:

> Truly my friends are both from rabbinical and military side [. . .]. In the army I have some non-Jewish friends, of whom are Christian Arabs, or Muslims. And since we are in the same environment of the army, we must set an example of living well together, so we really are not talking politics.

D., a long-term immigrant from Israel also describes mixed social networks, mostly of non-Jews, with whom he seems to have shallow relationships:

> I have the friends of everyday. My social life usually happens between seven and eight in the evening, which is the aperitif hour. I have bar friends [. . .]. Aren't they friends? These are not people I know from childhood. It means that one day, one of us will move two blocks away and adopt another bar, and he will start a new life. [. . .] I have friends here with whom I do not have much in common, I can talk to them, I am not close to them. I feel that they are part of my daily life, and their presence does me good.

H., an Israeli immigrant living in Paris for decades, also describes multicultural social networks, and implies that she attaches almost no importance to race or religion, except for avoiding religious Muslims:

> When you know people [. . .] you have Negro friends, you do not look at them, in fact you do not choose your friends by the color of their skin, you choose because you have things in common, you have a common culture, so of course my Arab friends are not Muslims, and are not religious. It is not exactly true, I have a Muslim girlfriend, but her culture is French and I feel with her as if she were my childhood friend, who grew up with me.

R., a native-born, refers to economic components: The rising cost of living which impacts his quality of life in Paris. He even considers immigrating to Marseilles: "I feel good [in Paris], but lately I ask myself what's the advantage of residing in Paris? Cost of living is high, we have to work hard and have no time to enjoy the city [. . .]. Maybe it will be better to live in Marseilles, where the weather it better, less expensive and life quality is better."

I asked him if these feelings stem from his Judaism; he denied this and claimed that all Parisians suffer from these problems: "It is a problem for each Parisian, Jewish or not. It is complicated since life is very expensive in Paris, and it's preferable to move to Provence." It is interesting to note that R. focused on the all-Parisian, economic issue. It is specifically surprising that he ignored the hardship of being Jewish in contemporary Paris, though in the street, before entering the restaurant where the interview took place, he took off his *Kippah* and put it on again after entering, which indicates some fear of being recognized as a Jew.

Rabbi Y., who serves as a military rabbi in Paris area expresses some frustration in his words regarding French people's perceptions of him as a foreigner and different, although he serves in their army. He mentioned his Jewish-Moroccan origin which makes him feel a constant stranger and a migrant, namely experience double marginality:

> They [his army friends] ask me who are you? Or when they say 'in your country' I say 'which country?' [. . .] they say 'Israel'. So, I tell them 'my country is here'. I am in the army, you can see which uniform I am wearing. How can you say that I am from Israel? If you look at my passport and see that I was born in Morocco, then you tell me that I am Moroccan? Even those with education have problems with Jews [. . .] I feel like an immigrant everywhere.

H., a long-term immigrant from Israel to Paris describes mutual alienation between native-born and new immigrants to the city. Implicitly, she resents newcomers. H. also uses words like "transparent" to describe inter-relations between them and herself:

> He is transparent, they are transparent. If they ask me for money I don't give them, the government should do it: It brought them, then it has to take care of them. I don't care about them. I have to take care of myself. I help people, if I know them personally [. . .]. You say hello to them they don't reply. They pass you by and don't see you [. . .]. Second-generation immigrants from Muslim countries they are everywhere, in offices, receptions etc. It is difficult to get information from them, they are not polite and do not smile at you like French people do.

I., a Parisian born in France, expressed feelings of fear when coming to the city center, which she had not experienced in the past: "Before that, I was never afraid, now I take care, where I sit, where I go, because I don't feel safe. When I take the metro, I do not feel very well."

4.4.2 Brussels

Rabbi A., from Brussels, expresses his feelings as an ultra-Orthodox immigrant, and says that although he understands the language and customs of the local native-born, he is still considered different, (probably since he is dressed differently): "I can definitely understand their language and more or less I understand their way of thinking, because I share a lot of their principles, let's say, but they are constantly trying to put me in a box, because if you look different you are supposed to be different. "

He further describes his encounters with Flemings and Walloons in Brussels as a rabbi; they are pleasant and he seems to like them:

> The Flemish side, yes, I think we worked together with many of these people: Organize big events, concerts or anything. They are a bit like 'Yekkes' [nickname for German Jews in Israel] you know, they are very efficient and they work well, they seem like very good people, nice people . . . and then the non-Jewish French they are also nice people.

B., an Israeli immigrant, describes Brussels as a pleasant city, but emphasizes recent changes regarding issues of security that can be felt:

> This is a very cosmopolitan city, very pleasant as a whole. The only thing is security: You can see soldiers near the court house, you see them walking in the streets, an unpleasant feeling. I never imagined that I would see soldiers at my school entrance. The non-Jewish teachers – it took them a long time to adjust. The worst thing is that we already got used to it, it seems reasonable and normal.

4.4.3 Antwerp

J., who emigrated from England many years ago, describes very warm interactions between herself and other residents in her neighborhood and particularly refers to solidarity with immigrants:

> I'm everybody's favorite [. . .], I'm their favorite neighbor. What I do notice though is that, you know, one lady who is lovely, she's from Tanzania, her husband is local, her children were brought up here. When something happens [. . .] we all go to each other straight away, we say 'is everything ok?' 'Can we help you?' 'Did this happen did that happen?' We help each other a lot. We may not speak to each other for a few months but if something happens [. . .].

G., an Israeli immigrant refers to non-Jewish Flemish women whom she meets in the school where she teaches. She describes them as pleasant people but her words imply that she does not have close relations with them, although she invites them to *Shabbat* dinner: "At school, there is the Flemish staff [. . .]. They are agreeable, very pleasant, interesting and I even invited them to our home for *Shabbat* [. . .]. Those who came to us for the first time were very excited about it. It was an interesting experience for them." When I asked her if she would go to their homes, if she were invited, she said she would definitely go: "I was not invited, but if I am, I have no problem to go [. . .], it does not intimidate me, in the religious or existential way." However, she describes Flemish people as very old fashioned regarding their educational systems. She implies that she perceives Flemish and Israeli cultures as very distant from each other: "The Flemish are very different from us, the Israelis, very much so [. . .] they are very old fashioned. The educational system has remained the same since the 18th century, regarding psychology, understanding children's soul and things like that."

L., another immigrant from Israel, expresses a feeling of alienation from the non-Jewish residents in Belgium in general, and in Antwerp – in particular. He partially masters the local language, as an almost sole attachment to them. His main connections are with the local Jewish community, including his use of various services, and actually it seems that he lives in an ethnic 'bubble':

> I am not a Belgian citizen, I do not feel Belgian. For me – residing in Antwerp means to have a pleasant exile, I am here for six years and can manage with Hebrew, English or French [. . .]. I even learned the local language, I understand it. There are Jewish stores, and the neighborhood in which I reside, it feels like living in a small Jewish city in Israel. Many Jews are around you, religious or secular – it does not matter.

In the interviews, some respondents consider emigration, as was also found in previous studies (see Ben-Rafael, 2017; DellaPergola, 2020a.). In the next section

I address possible future migration in the questionnaires, looking for various motives to emigrate, as well as present some quantitative findings.

4.5 Predispositions and Motives for Future Emigration

When asked (by country of origin and city of residence) to what extent respondents are sure they will remain in the country where they currently live, the only difference was in the rate of those who were sure and quite sure they would remain. Emerging from the comparison between native-born and immigrants, predisposition to remain in the city of residence was lower among the first group: 24% and 34%, respectively. Those residing in Antwerp, compared to respondents from Paris and Brussels, were more certain of remaining in their city of residence (41%, 27% and 26%, respectively). Thus, Jews living in Paris and Brussels appear to be less willing to remain in their current city of residence than are residents of Antwerp, where almost half are sure or quite sure they will remain. These findings, by country of origin and city, correspond, since those residing in Antwerp are mostly immigrants.

The next step was to analyze the specific motives to emigrate, should they consider to leave the country. In Table 5, I present differences between native-born and immigrants, followed by city of residence. These questions were answered by only two thirds of the sample, probably by only those who consider emigration.

When comparing between native-born and immigrants, native-born are more prone to emigrate, compared with those who are immigrants themselves. Although the general tendency to emigrate is slightly higher than medium extent (mean=3.69), there are some motives such as personal safety, spouse's desire, family in destination country and economic mobility which serve as push and pull factors for possible future emigration, particularly among native-born. Regarding children's education, there is no significant difference between native-born and immigrants, although among respondents from the first groups this motive is slightly higher. The most heterogeneous answers can be seen in the most prevalent two push (security and spouse) and one pull factor (family), among native-born. Evidently, this group considers these three motives as important in a similar manner (Table 5).

Motives for immigrating to another country that is not the country of origin, differ among residents of the three cities. In the overall measure of these motives, residents of Paris express the highest motivation to emigrate, compared to residents of Brussels and Antwerp (whose motivation levels are similar). While economic and professional motives are similar among respondents in three cities

Table 5: Motives for possible future migration, by two groups: Native-born and immigrants, T-test (1= Not at all; 5= To a very large extent).

Motives for migration	All N=293	Native-born N=158	Immigrants N=135	Significance of differences (2-tailed)
	Mean (SD)	Mean (SD)	Mean (SD)	
Economic mobility	3.68 (1.26)	3.82 (1.18)	3.51 (1.33)	*
Professional mobility	3.60 (1.33)	3.75 (1.23)	3.40 (1.43)	*
Children's education	3.79 (1.27)	3.88 (1.18)	3.68 (1.38)	n.s
Spouse's desire	3.89 (1.21)	4.08 (1.08)	3.66 (1.32)	**
Family in destination country	3.71 (1.36)	4.04 (1.08)	3.31 (1.55)	**
Emotional attachment to country of emigration	3.07 (1.34)	3.31 (1.30)	2.77 (1.33)	**
Personal safety	3.88 (1.21)	4.04 (1.09)	3.69 (1.32)	**
Index of motives for emigration (Cronbach's alpha=0.85)	3.72 (0.89)	3.89 (0.74)	3.51 (1.00)	**

*P<.05; **P<.01; n.s=not significant

and quite moderate, desire to give their children a better education elsewhere and the spouse's desire to emigrate are highest among Parisians; however, differences between the two Belgian cities are not that significant, with Brussels residents in 'the middle' between Paris and Antwerp. Family members living in emigration destination also constituted a major pull motive among Parisians, while this motive was only moderate in a similar manner among the residents of the Belgian cities. It is interesting to note that emotional attachment to country of destination is moderate and almost similar among respondents, as well as is the sense of personal safety in city of residence (Table 6).

Some interviewees addressed possible emigration in the future. They are aware of quite massive emigration of Jews from France recently, but they express their concerns, particularly former immigrants, regarding their own possible future emigration.

Rabbi M. from Paris expressed concern about future emigration from France. He is aware of probable decline in his status as a rabbi, of his responsibility for the community and difficulties of integration in a new place as a community rabbi:

> Who will know you? Even though I met everyone here. They do not care. I do not trust it. [. . .] At least I do not expect too much. [When] I came here I did expect to become a

Table 6: Motives for possible future migration, by city of residence, ANOVA (1= Not at all; 5= To a very large extent).

	All N=301	Paris N=172	Brussels N=90	Antwerp N=39	Significance of differences
	Mean (SD)	Mean (SD)	Mean (SD)	Mean (SD)	
Economic mobility	3.68 (1.26)	3.76 (1.24)	3.56 (1.22)	3.63 (1.39)	n.s
Professional mobility	3.60 (1.33)	3.70 (1.32)	3.50 (1.29)	3.43 (1.44)	n.s
Children's education	3.79 (1.27)	4.02^1 (1.16)	$3.60^{1,2}$ (1.29)	3.32^2 (1.47)	F=5.87**
Spouse's desire	3.89 (1.21)	4.07^1 (1.13)	$3.80^{1,2}$ (1.16)	3.45^2 (1.48)	F=4.19*
Family in destination country	3.71 (1.36)	4.07^1 (1.16)	3.44^2 (1.35)	2.87^2 (1.64)	F=15.92**
Emotional attachment to country of emigration	3.07 (1.34)	3.18^1 (1.29)	$3.08^{1,2}$ (1.32)	2.60^2 (1.48)	F=2.90*
Personal safety	3.88 (1.21)	3.97 (1.19)	3.88 (1.08)	3.51 (1.48)	n.s.
Index of motives for emigration (Cronbach's alpha=0.85)	3.72 (0.89)	3.85^1 (0.85)	$3.57^{1,2}$ (0.81)	3.24^2 (1.13)	F=8.42**

*P<.05; **P<.01; n.s=not significant

> rabbi of the Great Synagogue of France just nine years after I arrived here. It makes no sense at all. [. . .] So, I say to leave it [his mission as a rabbi], it's to run away [. . .] it scares me.

Rabbi Y. also claims that as a rabbi he is committed to his community and is prevented from emigrating: "So I as a rabbi say it is impossible to do that, because a rabbi must be within his community. And he cannot leave." However, he describes waves of emigration from Paris, and as result – a sharp decline in apartment prices:

> Recently, you see signs all over the city, 'sale', 'sale'. [. . .] Apartments were even more expensive than in Paris [in a settlement outside Paris], today since everyone is selling, prices fall. All those who sell are making '*Aliyah*' [immigration to Israel]. There are those who stay for work, but their wives and children are here in Israel. This is called '*Boeing Aliyah*'. So there are some who have left, they saw what was happening in France today.

D. is considering immigrating back to Israel despite his ambivalent attitude toward Israeli culture. He particularly refers to pull factors:

> I do not think I have plans [to emigrate from Paris and France]. The question is not on the agenda at the moment. Maybe I would like to live in Israel for a few months in a row, to see what draws me there so much. Because when I am there, with all the anger I have [towards Israel], I enjoy life, I live fully there, more than here. My good years were there, too. But let's not forget that I was also a young artist then.

A., a resident of Brussels and a native of Belgium, also talks about future emigration options. He mentions his age, 53, as making it difficult to move now and look for a new occupation. However, he notes that there is a possibility that he will immigrate with his family to Israel or Canada:

> When you are 53 which I am, it's a bit of a difficult moment, because if you move, the question is whether you will find professional activity, or you wait until you stop working and then you move. Possibly to Israel, or Canada or something like that. That's more likely, I think, one of these places, where there could also be a better future for the children.

M., a Belgian-born from Brussels as well, believes he will not emigrate; he perceives the country as his home and workplace and is aware, similarly to A., of immigration difficulties at the age of 45. However, perhaps in the future, with no commitment on his part, he sees his future in Israel:

> This is my place, this is my country, even though I'm Italian in my passport, but Belgium is my culture, I'm European. I was born here, I was raised here, I work here, I live here. So, to make a change at the age of 45 and to move, it's not easy. I think that one day, I might go to Israel and live there [. . .] it's my wish to go there and to make *Aliyah*.

F., a native-born from Brussels, finds it difficult to become an immigrant in the future. Perhaps she will immigrate to Israel, primarily due to climatic reasons, and only if she finds a job there:

> Indeed, I think there is small plot of land for me if something happens. I know that when I go to Israel I will feel 'at home.' But I find that today I'm too old to leave, I live here. I built my life here. [. . .] There, I need to have a job that will allow it. The sun, the beach, I think they have a different quality of life. It's safe. Maybe when I'm old. You never know.

C., a native of Belgium, describes his city, Antwerp today, as consisting mainly of ultra-Orthodox Jews, with whom he may well communicate in Yiddish, but thinks of emigrating from the city, mainly because his wife is interested in it and since he does not see a future there: "I will not continue here, I do not I know where I will go but it will be within a few more years, because my wife already wants to go to Brussels. [. . .] There is no future here, maybe for the Orthodox [. . .], but for the rest – there is no future here."

Although interviewees do not express urgent need to emigrate, they definitely consider it. Their main concerns are related to possible future occupational integration elsewhere – Israel or other countries.

4.6 Summary

This chapter focused on patterns of integration within the majority. Based on quantitative as well as qualitative data, the results indicate professional and economic relationship which constitute the main integration component among all participants, while social, communal and cultural interactions and relationship with non-Jewish residents are more limited.

In general, most interviewees are content with professional opportunities offered to them in France or Belgium, regardless of being native-born or immigrants, as well as with their city of residence. Interviewees noted that they had, or still have, occupations which are compatible with their skills and expectations; most of them work in their city of residence, and would not wish to practice their professional occupations elsewhere. However, very few express some disappointment with their mobility opportunities, particularly immigrants (short and long-term) and admit that elsewhere they might have fulfilled higher career ambitions.

Contrary to economic and professional integration, social, communal and cultural integration within the non-Jewish majority is more complex. Native-born Jews are slightly more integrated, compared with immigrants, as one should expect. Nevertheless, major quantitative differences were found in comparison by city of residence. It is obvious that those residing in Brussels appear to be those who reported on the most prevalent integration with non-Jews regarding social, economic, cultural, marital and communal components. Respondents residing in Paris and Antwerp, on the other hand, demonstrate almost similar patterns of segregation from the non-Jewish majority. Brussels' Jewish residents express a more pluralistic and assimilative pattern of integration, mostly social, communal and cultural, which probably reflects the city's cosmopolitan atmosphere. Nevertheless, very few respondents described their social networks as comprising a significant portion of non-Jews, as a result of their occupation or free choice. Almost all interviewees have mostly mixed social networks composed of Jews and few non-Jews.

The qualitative findings in this context can be placed on a spectrum: From those who feel more integrated within the non-Jewish majority, and as equal residents in each city, to partial integration, and in some cases – alienation and even fear, particularly in Paris and Brussels. Descriptions contained words such as 'pleasant city,' 'feel like an immigrant' (although the person has lived in Paris for decades), 'different,' and mentioned safety issues. It is interesting to note that integration was raised mainly by immigrants, short and old-term alike. A possible explanation is that integration issues are more relevant to immigrants, and to a lesser degree to native-born, although they are part of an ethnic minority. Native-born hardly referred to issues of integration in the interviews. Nevertheless, a quite recent sense of alienation and even fear were expressed by respondents, particularly among those from Paris and Brussels, which contradicts allegedly successful integration within the majority. These feelings are partially reflected in predisposition to emigrate and might explain patterns of socio-cultural segregation, which were described earlier.

Motives for emigration are a mixture of push and pull factors, such as personal safety or families in country of destination, respectively. As mentioned in the overview of this chapter, trends of emigration have already existed for almost a decade and seem to continue. Those residing in Antwerp feel safer, despite the fact that some of them, the Orthodox and some religious Israeli immigrants, have ethnic Jewish visibility. Antwerp residents seem to be subtler with regard to 'old' antisemitism, and the 'new' one is not yet felt as much as in Paris and Brussels.

Another component which adds to the dynamics of minority-majority interactions, and which was implicit in the interviews, is antisemitism and its various manifestations. In the next chapters I will present feelings and perceptions of both native-born and immigrants in each city, regarding antisemitism and its effect on future emigration.

Chapter 5
In Their Eyes: Antisemitism in Every-Day Life

5.1 Overview

This chapter will focus on contemporary antisemitism, as perceived on the macro level, and, particularly, as personally experienced by interviewees. It will begin by an overview which describes contemporary antisemitism in France and Belgium, based on previous findings. The 'findings' section will be based mainly on qualitative data regarding interviewees' perceptions of antisemitism and include a short quantitative paragraph, which will focus on respondents' attitudes towards possible future emigration, as a result of antisemitism. A summary will conclude this chapter.

Recently, Europe is facing an overall rise in racism and xenophobia: Growing racism and violence against minorities, fed by ultra-nationalism, antisemitism, and anti-Muslim hate. Coronavirus-inspired antisemitic expressions constitute forms of traditional Jew hatred and of conspiracy theories. So far, these accusations appear to be promoted mainly by extreme rightists, ultra-conservative Christian circles, Islamists, and to a minor extent, by the far-left, each group according to its narrative and beliefs, different conspiracy theories as well as the image of the Jew as a producer of diseases (Kantor Center, 2020). Furthermore, antisemitic harassment, includes antisemitic threatening comments in person, online and via email or texting, threats of violence and offensive gestures, targeting Jews as Jews. About a quarter of Jews in Europe are exposed to such harassment on annual basis. Antisemitic victimization is part of hate-motivated harassment of other ethnic minorities and migrants. Antisemitic harassment (28%) is similar in its scope to the levels experienced by European Roma and North African immigrants and their descendants. It is higher in its volume compared to minorities originating in Asia (15%) and sub-Saharan Africa (21%) (Staetsky, 2021).

The COVID-19 pandemic and the resulting reality dictated both the nature and extent of antisemitism in 2020, which was an unusually tense and turbulent year all over the world. Blaming Jews and Israelis for developing and spreading the coronavirus (or '*Judeovirus*'), was the main motive in this year's antisemitic manifestations. This notion is rooted in a deep fear of Jews or Israelis as spreaders of disease in both past and present. Lockdowns reduced encounters between Jews and their offenders, diminishing the number of violent incidents from 456 (in 2019) to 371 – a number typical for 2016–2018. No one was murdered this year for being Jewish, although any physical attack might end in a severe or

https://doi.org/10.1515/9783110698817-005

fatal outcome. In most countries a decrease was observed in violent incidents, attacks on both people and property, threats and arson, but the level of vandalism against Jewish property and institutions remained unchanged (Kantor Center, 2021).

Despite emancipation and legislation which enable Jews in France and Belgium to integrate well in their host societies, since 2000 the number of antisemitic incidents in France has increased and incidents have become more violent. A study analyzing attitudes of French Jews did not find any consensus among respondents regarding the rise in antisemitic incidents. This lack of consensus may derive first and foremost from new forms antisemitic stereotypes have assumed in France today, making comparisons to past data difficult. While almost no research has examined antisemitism in the form of anti-Zionist expressions, this has become the most prevalent form of antisemitism today, while previous forms of antisemitism which considered inter-relations among Jews and the majority in French society have diminished. Another possible explanation for lack of consensus about increasing antisemitism in France is related to the origin of these antisemitic acts in a small minority group whose activities do not find expression in opinion surveys. Classical forms of antisemitism are found among larger groups within the French Muslim population and among some rightwing supporters and less among extreme leftist groups. Thus, extreme forms of antisemitism in France, including the use of violence against Jews, are representative of a small portion of French population. Extreme marginal Muslim groups in France pose another security threat to French society in general and to French Jews in particular (Jikeli, 2017).

With regard to rising antisemitism in France, Wistrich claims that

> French Jewry is undoubtedly experiencing the most difficult decade in his postwar history – one that reflects the increasingly rotten state of French and European society. The broader social causes range from urban anomie, a seemingly uncontrollable Muslim immigration [. . .] and an ongoing crisis of French national identity   (Wistrich, 2015, 58).

A recent survey conducted by the American Jewish Committee (AJC, 2020) reveals that in Paris nearly three-quarters (73%) of general French majority and 72% of Jews consider antisemitism a problem that affects all French society. Almost half (47%) of the general population and 67% of Jewish respondents concede that the level of antisemitism in France is high, compared to 27% and 22% respectively, who say it is low. Half (53%) of the general population agree that antisemitism has been increasing, compared to 18% who think it has been decreasing. Among Jews, 77% say it has increased and only 12% that it has decreased. The extent of antisemitic attacks on France's Jewish community, the largest in Europe, is alarming: Seventy percent of French Jews report that they have been victims of at least one antisemitic incident in their lifetime; 64% have suffered antisemitic verbal abuse at least once, and 23% have been targets of physical violence on at least one occasion; among these 10% claim they were attacked several times (AJC, 2020).

The 687 antisemitic acts recorded in 2019 represent an increase of 27% compared to 2018. Remarkably, 60% of the overall 1142 racist hate crimes were antisemitic incidents. Incidents involving physical violence decreased by 17%, and threats increased by 50%. Moreover, two major cases involved desecration of Jewish cemeteries. In the context of the social unrest sparked by the Yellow Vests[8] movement, a number of antisemitic incidents were recorded, including Israel-related antisemitism (Kantor Center, 2020).

The number of antisemitic incidents recorded in France in 2020 by the Jewish Community Security Service in France (SPCJ), has declined by 50% compared to 2019. Physical assaults however, remained almost unchanged from 2019, despite nationwide lockdowns during the COVID-19 pandemic and decrease of activity in the Jewish community. Over three hundred (339) antisemitic incidents were recorded in 2020, significantly lower than the 687 in 2019 and 541 in 2018, and similar to figures for 2016 (335 incidents) and 2017 (311). The number of physical assaults remained almost unchanged, with 44 assaults in 2020 compared to 45 in 2019, despite three and a half months of COVID-19 lockdowns and restrictions, as well as the significantly lower activity in Jewish institutions. Decrease in antisemitic incidents was mainly noted in acts of vandalism, graffiti, insults and hate-mail, as opposed to virtual email (Kantor Center, 2021).

Belgian Jews do not perceive their country antisemitic, but they have experienced antisemitism related to the Israeli-Palestinian conflict; yet, despite their criticism of Israel, they do express solidarity with the Jewish state. At the same time, Belgian Jews feel a sense of belonging to and support for their country. Evidently, Belgium's current policy of multiculturalism towards minorities and immigrants has not brought about the dissolution of antisemitism. Rather, it is the respondents' conviction that hatred of Jews has increased over recent years (Ben-Rafael, 2017). However, Belgian Jews experience hostility in the streets to almost the highest degree in the EU, except for France, such as the deadly attack on the Jewish Museum on 24 May, 2014. Since 2001, Belgium has seen increase in the number of cases related to antisemitism. The number of antisemitic incidents more than doubled between 2017 and 2020, from 56 to 115. An increase of

---

8 The Yellow Vests movement or Yellow Jackets movement is a populist, grassroots protest movement for economic justice that began in France in October 2018 (Wikipedia, 2020).

32% was documented compared to 2019. It is clear that antisemitic discourse has become commonplace at all levels – from a call for war against Jews at a pro-Palestinian demonstration in Brussels to violence against *Haredi* (ultra-Orthodox) people in Antwerp. On five occasions, *Haredi* Jews, by definition extremely visible, were violently attacked by young Muslims or East Europeans. Antisemitism in Belgium has many manifestations; some are rooted in the extreme right while others come from the extreme left, and especially now, from the Muslim population. Another form is 'everyday antisemitism' in the form of stereotypes (Kantor Center, 2021).

As a result of rising antisemitism in the two countries, several studies (Cohen E. H., 2007; Cohen E. H, 2009; Cohen E. H., 2013) indicated a decreasing Jewish population in France, primarily due to emigration, mainly to Israel, but also to Canada, the US, and other countries. Immigration to Israel, after surpassing 2,000 annually for several years, actually increased to a historical peak of 6,627 in 2015, and lowered again to 2,431 in 2018, for a total of over 48,000 between 2001 and 2018. Jewish emigration was also directed toward other western countries and reflected a continuing sense of uneasiness in face of antisemitism, in part stemming from Islamic fundamentalism and terrorism, as well as economic considerations. Assuming Israel attracted half to two-thirds of the total who departed France, between 72,000 and 96,000 Jews and family members emigrated from France since 2001. Some of these returned to France in the meantime, thus reducing the impact of net migration (DellaPergola, 2020a; Pohorils, 2017).

Significant emigration from Belgium since 2000, reflects growing concerns about Islamization, terrorism and antisemitism, similarly to the situation in Paris: Around 224 Belgian Jews immigrated to Israel in 2014, and 242 in 2015 (Ben-Rafael, 2017; DellaPergola, 2017).

5.2 Perceptions regarding Antisemitism: "The Jews, They Are Not Part of the Celebration"

Although not asked specifically about antisemitism, just "How does it feel to be a Jew in your city of residence?" some interviewees referred to the macro level, offering some explanations for the sources of new antisemitism while others focused on their personal experience.[9] I will present the qualitative findings according to city of residence and between immigrants and native-born.

---

9 The quote in the title is from an interview with D. from Paris.

5.2.1 Paris

On the macro level, Rabbi Y. (long-term immigrant from Morocco) relates contemporary antisemitism to young Arabs born in France, who act differently towards minorities, unlike the first generation of their parents who arrived in the 1950s and 1960s: "Antisemitism today is attributed to Arabs, not those who immigrated to France in the first immigration waves [in the 1950s and 1960s]. With them there was no problem. Today it is the young people, who were born in France, and they have no idea what a Jew is."

H., a long-term immigrant from Israel, describes antisemitism in Paris as being directed primarily at Jewish children. She believes that antisemitism exists among Muslims but also acknowledges antisemitism among native-born Christian French, who are more careful in expressing it, as racism in France is not acceptable:

> The first who feel antisemitism are Jewish children. [. . .] It is easier to persecute a Jew, once they are children, because here you have the Islam that is growing, and the young children do not understand who is Muslim [. . .]. The French have always been antisemitic. Racism and antisemitism are considered shame in France. Today, racism is such a great shame that antisemitism is considered less [. . .], so the children are harmed, beaten and so on.

O., who was born in France, relates to native-born French and their attitudes towards Jews as part of their xenophobia, which is now intensifying mainly against Muslims. Antisemitism, in his perception, is related to increase in Muslim population which accelerates expressions of antisemitism, anti-Zionism and Israel:

> I have always said that, and I still think the French people are basically frightened by strangers, if not frightened, they don't like them. When the Arabic people came, Jewish people they are quieter. [. . .] Now, that the Arabic people had grown so much, they hate the Jews [as well], and their antisemitism has expanded much more. I think that antisemitism rising in France is both antisemitism against Jews, Zionism and Israel.

From a personal point of view, D., an immigrant from Israel, notes that he experienced incidents of antisemitism and learned to recognize them over the years as a long-term immigrant: "Regarding antisemitism I also went through all sorts of processes. I do not deny, I do not say there is no antisemitism, but they [Israelis in Israel] do not recognize antisemitism because they do not identify the nuances. [. . .] Now I do recognize it."

When I asked D. how he recognized antisemitism, he described it in harsh words such as being "attacked" in various religious and political contexts, alongside Jewish "otherness"; it is not clear whether the situation is perceived by him as a positive or problematic:

> When I start a conversation with someone, then he tries to take me to his 'field,' and he throws me a word here and a word there, and I know where it leads: If he attacks from the religious point of view, or from the political, in both cases I know where it's going. [. . .] It is similar to living in one big nudist camp, and there are those who come to a nudist camp with a bathing suit – it's the Jews. They are not part of the celebration.

N., a native-born, claims that "As long as time passes we feel less secure." S., a long-term immigrant from Morocco, describes antisemitism in 'softer' terms and does not explicitly use the word 'antisemitism.' However, he also notes that today a Jew who wears a *Kippah* in Paris could be in a problematic situation: "I feel less secure lately. I kept walking for decades with a *Kippah* on the street [. . .]. Since the terrorist attack on the Club de Batklan, in 2015 [. . .] I do not feel safe. I think that is what happens to everyone. Now I walk with a hat."

5.2.2 Brussels

With regard to contemporary antisemitism, Brussels residents voice similar perceptions to those expressed by Parisian interviewees, although in different contexts. Interviewees from Brussels also describe a change in inter-relations with the majority and some relate to their childhood as Jewish children versus the contemporary situation.

On the macro level, B., an immigrant from Israel, relates to new antisemitism, compared with the old one as subtler, although it is not clear from her words who anti-Semites are, Muslims or Christians native-born: "Before World War II it [antisemitism] was more blatant. Today they are more careful, they do not want to be caught antisemitic."

New feelings of fear, following recent terrorist attacks in Brussels, were described by A., a native-born: "We feel more threat, I guess everybody will tell you that as a first thing [. . .]. Until a few years ago, I never felt much threat, now I do, after the Brussels shooting and bombs."

Another native-born, F., also used the word 'fear' to describe the situation in the city, which she says causes Jews to emigrate from it:

> People are more scared. [. . .] In the Jewish community there are a lot of people who immigrated to Israel or somewhere else to the United States, because I think they are scared. And it's true [. . .] when you walk downtown you're scared. I visited the center frequently I was never afraid. I always felt safe. But, but today I'm scared.

M., also a native-born, describes the change regarding his children participating in the Zionist Youth movement. He says that Jewish symbols should be hidden or disguised in public, something that did not exist during M.'s childhood:

For instance, the kids in the youth movement, *Hanoar Hatziyoni* [Zionist Youth, a youth movement] they play in the building, they have their activities. But if they go to the park, it's better nowadays not to wear the shirt with a *Magen David* [David's shield, a Jewish symbol on the Israeli flag]. You don't have to hide yourself as a Jew, but you don't have to show it, either. It's worse now. Something that happens lately, because when I was myself in the youth movement like thirty years ago, we could go outside with the shirt, with a *Magen David*. The only threat you had at that time, was someone bad in the street who could come and start to argue with you, but nowadays you've got an additional threat which is the terrorist.

Rabbi A., an immigrant from Argentina, describes blatant antisemitism in Brussels towards his children, mainly due to their ethnic appearance as ultra-Orthodox Jews: "My kids if they wear *Kippah*, there are taxi drivers that yell at them 'Palestine, Palestine' or '*Juifs, Juifs*' stuff like that, so I feel very bad, it's for my kids not to me. Sometimes they shout at me but mostly to my kids."

5.2.3 Antwerp

In Antwerp antisemitism seems to be somewhat different than in Paris and Brussels. J., a native-born, refers to old antisemitism versus the new. According to her, some locals are antisemitic in a subtle way, and attributes the manifestations of new antisemitism to Muslims:

They are trying blame it on Muslims [. . .]. I think that in fact it fell into the laps of everyone, it's fantastic, 'cause now it's all the Muslims who are antisemitic. [. . .] It makes it a lot easier. The people who always have been [. . .] antisemitic [. . .] It's very subtle.

J. notes that she did not personally experience antisemitism, except for very subtle insinuation in the words "with you Jews": "I personally never experienced antisemitism. It's something that is very typical, you know, people when they talk they'll say [. . .] "*Bij jolle*". It's like slang in Dutch 'with you' people it's like this or like that." Nevertheless, as the interview went on, she mentioned a case in which her daughter was involved at the school, where most pupils were non-Jews:

She [her daughter,] was always top of her class but I brought them [my children] up so that they're not allowed to brag. What would happen is that [. . .] I would get the mothers coming up to me and going: 'Oh, she's very smart' and 'Ah, she's clever.' They would get the boys at school to grab her report from her and over the years it was the same mothers, some would say: 'Yes, with you people it's very easy, you know, you tend to be smart.' And I used to go: 'Yes that's true.'

When I asked J. why she did not see those words as a compliment to her daughter, she replied: "Well, it's not a compliment. From them it's not a compliment. It's derogatory."

L., a relatively short-term Israeli immigrant (six years), notes that he did not notice antisemitic incidents, although he is aware that of course this situation may change: "I hear neither about problems nor about conflicts or unusual antisemitic incidents. [Jews here] do not feel anxious every second that someone would throw something at them or curse them. It is very, very calm. However, it can change every second."

When I pointed out to him that in Paris interviewees noted that they avoided wearing a *Kippah* in public, he claimed that

> I also do not walk around with a *Kippah* outside of this place [the school where he works] in Antwerp, but I have never walked around with a *Kippah*. Even ten years ago, when I was traveling in Europe, or anywhere else in America, I would wear a hat [. . .]. I do not want to show off my Judaism. I have no interest in standing out as a Jew.

G., an emissary teacher from Israel (1.5 years in Antwerp), also says that she feels secure and even lets her children walk around the city in Jewish clothing: "All my kids were walking around town shopping, I did not feel insecure. We feel very safe, sometimes a little too much, because my children find it difficult not to walk around with a *Kippah* and tassels outside, against the instructions we receive, say from the security officer."

Contrary to L. and G., who are relatively short-term Israeli immigrants in Antwerp and describe it as non-antisemitic, C., native-born Belgian, describes a specific event that took place about a decade ago though, but he vividly describes it as if it happened yesterday. The event has been described by him as violent and as an example of Muslim takeover recently:

> Muslims here are getting stronger and stronger while obeying the rules to a small extent. For example, at least 10 years ago I left work. It was winter, and I rode my bike on the street. There was a car that come like crazy so I told him 'oh, quiet, sir,' so he opens the window and tells me in Flemish: 'All the dirty Jews should be killed'.

5.3 Antisemitism and Future Emigration

The quantitative results (Table 7) point at the same pattern that emerged from the qualitative analysis: Paris residents in particular, and to some extent, Brussels residents, compared with those from Antwerp, report on antisemitism as a possible push factor when considering future immigration to another country.

When comparing between native-born and immigrants, the first group is the one more predisposed to emigrate as a result of antisemitism (mean=4.10, standard deviation=1.07; mean=3.48; standard deviation=1.41, respectively). Since two thirds of Parisian respondents are native-born, 54% are native-born in Brussels, while those from Antwerp are mostly immigrants (66%), these quantitative results correspond with each other. Namely, those from Paris and native-born are more prone to emigration, compared with Brussels and particularly Antwerp, and more than immigrants.

Table 7: Antisemitism as a push motive for future migration, by city of residence – ANOVA (1 = Not at all; 5 = To a very large extent).

	All	Paris	Brussels	Antwerp	Significance of differences
	Mean (SD)	Mean (SD)	Mean (SD)	Mean (SD)	
Antisemitism in current country of residence	3.81 (1.28)	4.06^1 (1.16)	3.64^2 (1.26)	3.17^2 (1.51)	**F=9.09

**P<.01.

5.4 Summary

Antisemitism seems to be part of everyday life, particularly in Paris and Brussels. Some consider 'new' antisemitism as stemming from second-generation Muslim immigrants, others note that local native-born were and still are antisemitic but in a more 'politically correct' way. Interviewees seem to be more prone to blame Muslim immigrants with 'new' antisemitism and indirectly – the 'old' one, as they are more cautious of blaming native-born Christian French or Belgian people.

As for personal experience of antisemitism in every-day life, words such as 'insecure' and 'attack' are mentioned in the interviews, and reflect a change in feelings of trust in the majority. These feelings are shared by both immigrants who came to France decades ago from the Maghreb countries, and native-born Jews. Interviewees residing in Brussels, both native-born and immigrants, describe antisemitism and its manifestations as a new phenomenon, often frightening and sometimes blunt. The native-born remember their childhood nostalgically, or their young adulthood as being much more harmonic with regard to inter-relations with the majority. Contrary to Parisian interviewees who mainly attribute new antisemitism to Muslim immigrants, it is not clear to whom those from Brussels refer: Muslims or native-born Christian Belgians. Interviewees from Antwerp, mainly Israelis, describe feelings of security, although aware of risks in wearing a *Kippah* or other Jewish symbols among non-Jews. A native-born from Antwerp, elaborated, by attributing antisemitism to both Christian native-born and Muslims. However, she says that Christians are more sophisticated and 'hide' behind new antisemitism and the Muslims, in this regard. Furthermore, native-born are more aware of antisemitism in Brussels and in Antwerp, compared with immigrants, particularly those from Israel. A possible explanation to this finding might be that Israelis, most of whom are recent immigrants, are part of the majority in their homeland and thus less sensitive to antisemitism compared with native-born and Jewish immigrants from other countries, such as the Maghreb, who have experience as minorities. Perceptions regarding antisemitism, found primarily through the interviews, correspond with previous findings, regarding current waves of antisemitism in France and in Belgium (Kantor Center, 2020; Kantor Center, 2021).

Therefore, rising antisemitism effects feelings of fear, alienation and predisposition for future emigration, particularly among those who are supposed to feel attached to and safe in their countries of birth and cities of residence.

Chapter 6
Changes in Jewish Communal Organizations Structure, Involvement and Social Networks

6.1 Overview

This chapter will focus on participants' macro and micro perceptions regarding ethno-demographic, denominative and organizational changes in local Jewish communities as well as their own involvement in them. I base my analysis on qualitative and quantitative data, which provide a dynamic profile of these communities, their contemporary structure and vitality, as well as personal experience and involvement in the local Jewish communities and the structure of social networks.

I will begin by general description of Jewish communities in France and Belgium and the changes they went through in last decades, based on previous studies. This section will be followed by analysis of interviewees' perceptions beginning with macro perceptions of the three communities focusing on each one of them, followed by description of participants' micro point of view regarding their community involvement and social networks.

The CRIF (Representative Council of Jews of France), currently the country's primary Jewish umbrella group, was established in 1944 to serve as the political representative of the organized Jewish community. In 1986, the CRIF became the French affiliate of the World Jewish Congress. Today, the CRIF is the official organization representing French Jewry vis-à-vis the government, representing more than 70 organizations. Despite its size, the CRIF does not handle religious issues, which are still, according to the model set down by Napoleon, the responsibility of the *Consistoire Israelite de France* (World Jewish Congress, 2020). The estimate affiliation rate does not refer to central Jewish community institutions, but rather measures a more generic rate of involvement and participation in Jewish community activities (DellaPergola and Staetsky, 2020).

Only in Britain is the cost of Jewish schooling paid for by the state in many cases, whereas in France, for example, Jewish schools require tuition fees. Thus, only 24% of the parents, aged 20 to 54, send their children to a Jewish school or Jewish kindergarten (Graham, 2018). Furthermore, with its highly centralized system and predominantly Catholic population, the concept of citizenship is at the core of education in France. State education is considered the key to political freedom and to national identity, achieved particularly through linguistic

https://doi.org/10.1515/9783110698817-006

unification. The strongest normative pillar of French political philosophy is the separation of state and church, and thus, education is secular. Education in France is selective and based upon a rigid system of examinations that dictates the content and method of instruction. The goal is to offer pupils equal opportunity in knowledge acquisition. Freedom in the choice of public schools is highly restricted; parents are allowed to send their children only to schools located in their neighborhood. Alongside the public-school system, however, there are private schools that serve various groups in the population. Government support for these schools is dependent on the extent of the government's pedagogical involvement (Gross, 2006).

All major Zionist organizations are active in France and there are several local youth movements. Despite the organizational and communal Jewish vitality in France, only around 40% of the community is officially affiliated with, or are members of synagogues or Jewish organizations. Alongside assimilation, there is also a noticeable tendency toward religious revival, including a growing ultra-Orthodox community (World Jewish Congress, 2020).

Paris is the center of Jewish organization and communal activities in France. In Paris alone, there are more than 20 Jewish day schools, as well as multiple kindergartens and religious seminaries (World Jewish Congress, 2020).

Paris is also the center of the intellectual and cultural life of French Jewry: Conferences, colloquia, exhibitions, and other Jewish-content activities. Paris is the home of the largest Jewish library in Europe, of *Alliance Israélite Universelle*, another very important library devoted to Yiddish literature, *Bibliothèque MEDEM*, as well as of significant archival collections regarding the history of Jews in France. *The Centre de Documentation Juive Contemporaine* and its *Memorial des Martyrs Juifs* is one of the leading memorial sites for the Holocaust created after World War II. Yet, most research carried out on Judaism, its history, its culture, and Jewish languages is mostly conducted in institutes of higher education. Numerous teams at the *Centre National de la Recherche Scientifique* deal with research focusing on the "science of Judaism and Jewishness." A dozen Paris universities have departments or courses of study devoted to Hebrew, to other Jewish languages, or more general, to teaching and research related to Judaism and Jewish studies. Paris today is one of the main centers for Jewish intellectual life in the Diaspora (Jewish Virtual Library, 2021).

The Jewish population in Belgium is largely bi-nodal, based in Brussels and Antwerp which, although just 45 kilometers away from each other, are worlds apart in terms of religious observance. In Antwerp there is large *Haredi* (ultra-Orthodox) presence, so respondents there are more likely to follow each of the six practices than the more secular Jews of Brussels, in most cases by a considerable margin (Graham, 2018).

All issues of Jewish religion in Belgium are concentrated, since 1891, under an umbrella organization called the *Consistoire Central Israélite de Belgique* or by its more familiar name: *Consistoire Juive,* a community body that operates to this day (Schreiber, 2000).

In countries like Italy, Germany, and Austria, the central or local Jewish community organizations effectively cover the vast majority of the known Jewish population (70–80%) and also keep relatively well organized and updated Jewish community registers. Belgium, with a similar estimated level of affiliation is different: Due to the divided character of the Jewish population between the more secular center in Brussels and the more traditional one in Antwerp, no dominant central body can really claim control of the whole Jewish public (DellaPergola and Staetsky, 2020).

The constitutional recognition of minority religions means that the various levels of government welcome independent schooling systems and provide funding for religious schools (World Jewish Congress, 2020). The proportion of children currently attending a Jewish school or kindergarten, among respondents aged 20 to 54 is the highest among Belgian respondents (46%). Both Belgium and the UK exhibit levels that are notably higher than all the other countries. In the British case this is presumably because of free tuition, but this cannot explain the Belgian position. Belgium is thus the European country in which Jews are most likely to send their children to Jewish schools (Graham, 2018). Earlier study (Gross 2006) describes the Belgian educational system as enabling all ethnic groups to choose where they want to send their children. Belgium is a federal state composed of three language-related communities (German, French, and Flemish) that are responsible for cultural matters, education, and health. The Belgian constitution guarantees the separation of church and state together with freedom of religion and public worship. Schools in Brussels used to be dominated by the francophone orientation. However, in recent years the parents have demanded special departments for teaching Flemish. Belgium's educational system is neutral. All public schools are obliged to offer a choice between instruction according to a recognized religion, or secular universalistic instruction. Freedom of education guarantees parents free choice of a school that subscribes to their philosophical or religious convictions. Furthermore, any student in a public school can take two hours of Jewish studies with a special Jewish studies teacher who receives his or her salary from the government. This encourages Jewish parents to send their children to public schools. The official status of the private Jewish schools is "recognized" (*reconnu*), and they receive government support only if they agree to government inspection of the general studies curriculum and teaching methods. The Jewish community in Brussels is largely secular and sends its children to public schools or to the two less religious among the three private schools (Gross, 2006). Thus, it seems that sending their children to Jewish schools is a more recent pattern, when comparing Graham (2018) and Gross' (2006) studies.

Both Brussels and Antwerp have institutes for higher Jewish studies attached to a university. Brussels, which is the capital of the European Union, also hosts the headquarters of the European Jewish organizations. Above all, Belgian Jewry supports Jewish educational institutions, including high-level secondary schools (Ben-Rafael, 2017).

Belgium has 45 active synagogues, 30 of which – all Orthodox – are in Antwerp. Several synagogues also serve as houses of study for the ultra-Orthodox sects present in the city. The Antwerp community has its own chief rabbi. There are more than 10 synagogues in Brussels, including two Reform congregations – one of them English-speaking – and three *Sephardi* synagogues. The chief rabbi of Belgium is appointed by the community and officiates at the country's main synagogue, *La Régence,* which was re-dedicated in 2008 as the Great Synagogue of Europe. Both the chief rabbi and the main synagogue are funded by the government. Brussels has also a special Jewish communal lay center, the *Centre Communautaire Laïc Juif* (World Jewish Congress, 2020).

There are seven Jewish schools in Antwerp and three in Brussels, from kindergarten to secondary schools. The great majority of Jewish children in Antwerp are educated in the Jewish school system and receive an intensive religious education. Antwerp also has several yeshivas. There are six Jewish youth organizations in Belgium, in Brussels in particular and Antwerp such as *Bnei Akiva* (religious-Zionist youth movement, L. L.) and *Hanoar Hatsioni.*(youth movement of secular youth) Whereas in Brussels alone there are also *Hashomer Hatzair* and *Jeunesse Juif Laïque-* among others (World Jewish Congress, 2020).

6.2 Dynamic Macro Structure and Vitality of the Three Jewish Communities

Respondents in the present study were asked to describe, through the questionnaires, the various Jewish communities in their city of residence. According to a very high percentage of the respondents, each of the three cities has a community of native-born Jewish residents. Diasporic communities of Jewish immigrants from Israel or other countries were much less prevalent, with only half the respondents reporting on their existence. With respect to communities of Jewish immigrants from Israel, one-fifth of the respondents did not know how to respond, while regarding communities of Jewish immigrants from other countries than Israel, more than a third did not know (Table 8).

A comparison between native-born and immigrant respondents revealed one significant difference, whereas 70% of the immigrants reported that there is a diasporic Jewish-Israeli community in their city of residence, compared to 43% of native-born respondents. When compared by city of residence, it is interesting to note that regarding native-born Jewish community, 80% from Paris and 82% from Brussels acknowledge its existence, compared with 72% among those residing in Antwerp. As for diasporic Jewish Israeli immigrants, less than a third (31%) of the Parisians reported having this community in their city, whereas in Brussels and Antwerp respondents are aware of the existence of such communities to much higher percentages (69% and 90% accordingly), which reflects the actual presence of this group in Paris (see also Chapter 2). Finally, over a half of the respondents in Paris (57%) and Antwerp (54%) wrote that Jewish immigrants from other countries reside in their city, compared with 46% among those from Brussels.

Table 8: Jewish communities in city of residence (percentages).

	No	Yes	Do not know
Native-born local Jews	10	80	10
Jewish-Israeli immigrants	26	54	20
Immigrant Jews from countries other than Israel	13	52	35

Interviewees who expresses their perceptions regarding macro issues of their Jewish communities were mostly native-born and long-term immigrants (more than 15 years in the host country). The qualitative data is arranged according to city of residence.

6.2.1 Paris

From his status as the rabbi of one of the largest synagogues in Paris, although being a long-term immigrant from Israel, Rabbi M. provides a macro description of the Jewish community in the city, as united and as long-established, which undergoes significant changes regarding its inner ethnic and denominative structure. The rabbi further elaborates and describes a more complex picture of the Jews of France, which North Africans occupying a more prominent place in recent decades. The *Ashkenazi,* according to his description, remained a minority among French Jewry, who have less affiliation with current Jewish community:

> The Jewish community here is very unique, they call it French Jewry. I mean, when you say French Jewry, they tried to break down all the walls of *Ashkenazi* and liberals or conservatives [. . .] The community has changed, I think, especially since the sixties, compared with the community of the *Consistoire*, that was founded in the nineteenth centuries by Napoleon. [On the current president of the *Consistoir* L. L]: "He is from North Africa. Previously, Rothschild families were the presidents for generations. Currently it's new now that they are *Sephardi*. But it can also be the transformation that the community is going through [. . .]. Liberals are out, although we have [. . .] a very open Orthodox community [. . .]. This means that liberal Judaism accounts for maybe a tenth of a percent of all Judaism here. The Conservative movement, who established recently, is also about a quarter of a percent [. . .]. "They [the *Ashkenazi]* are very rich. They got rich after the war, everything had to be built [. . .] it's a wealth that has no end. They donate to Israel, then to the community here [. . .]. They are very involved in the community.

S., a long-term immigrant from Morocco, also describes the Jewish inner ethnic structure change – from *Ashkenazi* to North African mainly, as a result of aging processes among the first, who were also apparently not religious according to him:

> After the Holocaust in the 1950s until the late 1990s, everything there was Jewish [. . .]. *Ashkenazi* Jews were not involved in Jewish life. Their community naturally dwindled. They did not immigrate to Israel, nor did they immigrate to America, they stayed in Paris, and lived here, grew old and died here. North Africans bought and held their business, and now Pakistani Afghans have taken it, and the Chinese.

S., also attaches great importance to the Jewish community in Paris, which since the 1970s has provided a solution for those who needed it. He also points out that the community is the unifying factor by having many inner institutions for the whole community, immigrants and native-born, in Paris or elsewhere in France:

> The Jewish community in France, brought them some security. Not financial, but a framework that you feel you are a Jew, and you have someone to turn to [. . .] take care of each other [. . .]. And this generation that left the Arab countries, which were really prone to disaster [. . .] found some shelter [. . .]. Everyone found themselves here: A school, a synagogue, some *Kosher* food [. . .]. If not, this whole population would have been lost [. . .] traditionally.

Furthermore, S. describes the inner changes that the Jewish community in Paris underwent, from a process of assimilation in the 1970s to the 1990s, through a significant establishment and reinforcement of Jewish culturally and religiously organizations. S. also elaborates regarding the revival of the Parisian community, particularly among young people. He seems to be very proud of the Jewish flourishing in Paris, and claims that it is unique to the city:

In Boulogne [. . .] in the seventies and the eighties, there was not a single grocery store. There was no restaurant, there was one synagogue in the north of the city, which was almost empty. Today you need to be a candidate to get a place and find a place to sit and need a subscription to enter. You have to wait five or six years until you have a place in the synagogue. [. . .] Today, there are all kinds of arrangements in phonetics everyone can read, everyone reads in Hebrew, everyone sings in Hebrew, and their children who did not even come to schools and synagogues – today they are full of children and adults yes teenagers and even above that, the average age in synagogues is very low. They read in the *Torah*, every student knows how to do it today.

R., a native-born, reinforces S.'s perceptions regarding the vitality and many institutions belonging to the Jewish community in the city: Independent synagogues, *Mikvehs* (ritual baths), restaurants and a community center:

There are synagogues but they are independent, they are not dependent on the Jewish umbrella organization. There is a community center, there is a *Habad* house, there are many things. The community is very active. They organize a lot of things every holiday. On *Sukkot* [The Feast of Tabernacles] there are a lot of organized community meals, on Hanukkah there is a public candle lighting. Every day there are parties for children on Hanukkah in every synagogue.

6.2.2 Brussels

Rabbi A. who is a *Habad* emissary born in Argentina, described the Jewish community in Brussels as composed mainly of Holocaust survivors and their descendants from Poland mainly, and today Jewish immigrants from other countries: "I think it's [Jewish community] mainly polish. Than throughout the years there are newcomers from England or other places, but mainly it's a very polish community."

A., a native-born, reports on some Israeli-Jews in Brussels and another small group who emigrated from France mainly due to economic motives. Finally, A. referred to groups of ultra-Orthodox in the city, and he said there were few in the past and those who remained, sought out ultra-Orthodox communities in Antwerp or other countries:

Then there is a small minority of Israelis, [. . .] or other people coming from other countries. [There are] a few French now, because they have come here, not all but some of them for economic reasons. Traditionally it's not been a very Orthodox community, and maybe those few who are or were – left the city. Because they don't have many peers, services and a community, so I guess for them there's not much point to stay here. They went to Antwerp or London, maybe a few to Switzerland as well, or New York. They are very mobile, the ultra-Orthodox.

A. describes the Jewish community today as strong and organized, including three solid schools, one of which was probably closed due to its location in a neighborhood that was previously Jewish:

> I think it's quite well organized over all, you have strong Jewish schools. I think we lost one, there were three . . . but the other two are doing very well. We lost one because they were in a very bad neighborhood. In the past this was a place where you have all the business of rugs and clothing, mostly Jewish.

Another aspect that characterizes and distinguishes the Jewish community in Brussels, according to A., is the existence of active youth movements, and a Jewish radio station, which in his opinion does not exist in other European countries: "Well, we spoke about the . . . youth movements which are I think quite active and successful. Otherwise there is a radio station which is not often the case I believe, in Europe or anywhere." In addition, M., another native-born notes that the Jewish community is mainly secular, since there are very few Orthodox Jews living there, who prefer Antwerp as a community that provides Jewish education to their children. Furthermore, he describes the local Jewish community as having few Jewish institutions, such as synagogues, *Kosher* restaurants and *Kosher* supermarkets, compared to Paris:

> Very few of them [Orthodox Jews] live in Brussels, and those who live in Brussels do not feel comfortable with the schools, because they do not have enough Jewish schools in Brussels, so they go in any case to Antwerp, they go and study there. People want to go to a synagogue, has to live close to a synagogue, and you don't have a synagogue everywhere in Brussels, whereas in Paris you've got lots of possibilities. In Brussels I think we have only one or two *Kosher* restaurants, there's two *Kosher* supermarkets in Brussels.

T., short-term Israeli immigrant, also described an organized Jewish community, but from a more secular-social aspect, which holds many events and is associated with organizations such as the JNF [Jewish National Foundation]: "There are many organizations in the Jewish community, and we have many activities, such as a sport day to which all youth movements and the JNF delegates arrive to these events."

6.2.3 Antwerp

C., a native-born, points to the composition of the Jewish community in the city, and focused on the structure and visibility of the ultra-Orthodox community: "In 1957 at that time there were no religious people. Today you only see the wigs and the black. *Shomrei Hadath* [keepers of religion] are not free but very free relatively to *Machzikey Hadath* [holders of religion]." In addition, C. describes other new communities in the city, Moroccans, Israelis and Georgian-Jews:

> There are people here, *Sephardi*, who came from Morocco or come from Israel and live here. There is a Spanish community, they have nothing to do with the religious here, it is a different world. They have a synagogue here, they are usually nice [. . .]. The Georgians are new community here, about ten years old, also a different world, they have nothing to do with the religious, they are a closed community.

J., long-term immigrant from England, describes the change in the structure of the Jewish community in the city, since World War II, with regard to denominations. From a mixed and mostly non-religious population to an ultra-Orthodox population. As a result, non-religious Jews are also fluent in Yiddish:

> I know from my father that before the war you didn't have all those ultra-Orthodox, that's something that happened after the war. I think they came primarily from Romania, maybe from Hungary. It was different. Before the war it was much more mixed [. . .]. I do think it's a community that were for a very long time non-religious. Ultra-Orthodox lived incredibly well, it's one of the rare places where, you know, we all spoke Yiddish. Today you will not find non-religious people who speak Yiddish.

In his description, L., a relatively new immigrant from Israel, elaborates regarding additional changes that have taken place in the structure of the Jewish community in the city. He describes the interaction between the various Jewish groups in the city as harmonious, mainly through the city's diamond exchange:

> In the past, everyone worked together in the diamond exchange: *Haredi*, secular, religious. Everyone knew everyone, and through the work connections were formed. There's one more community, the *Sephardi* [. . .] who came here in the 1930s, fled Lebanon, Syria, or all sorts of places. The source of the Spanish community is Portuguese Jews who came here after the deportation, came to the Netherlands. [. . .] The Georgians came from all sorts of places: Some from Georgia directly, some immigrated to Israel and then came here [. . .], some came from Barcelona [. . .] from all sorts of places. But today it is a very large community, they have a rabbi, a school. [. . .] All the shops you see here, near the central train station belong to the Georgian community. They are mainly engaged in the trade of jewelry, diamonds, gold, and all kinds of things like that.

L offers a particularly detailed description of the various organizations in the Jewish community. He refers mainly to the dominant communities in the city and emphasizes their organizational integrity concerning food, religion practices and education, as well as those regarding life circles' ceremonies: Branched *Kosher* arrays, synagogues, educational systems from kindergarten to high school and beyond. From L.'s words it seems that he perceives the local Antwerp Jewish community as extremely vivid and organized.

> The whole cycle of life exists here, [. . .] from a *Kosher* system, [. . .] a community rabbinate system which deals with the issue of marriage and divorce, inheritance and burial. This whole institution of court and rabbinate. There is a burial society for this group, a burial society for the other group. Of course, there are synagogues, there are at least forty-five, fifty synagogues in a very small area [. . .]. Everything related to the subject of education: From *Talmud Torah* [school for religious studies], Jewish kindergartens, and Jewish dormitories, until high school graduation. There is no Jewish university. Will not be here either, but there are 'high Yeshivas' [. . .] here as well.

Although L. describes a very vibrant Jewish community, it characterizes probably the ultra-Orthodox community, since he claimed that university will not be established by the Jewish community in Antwerp. However, M. describes processes of the weakening of Jewish identity between the generations, among some members of the community, who do not belong to the ultra-Orthodox communities. The school he runs he defines as a non-religious Jewish school, but a traditional Zionist one: "It belongs to the traditional, non-religious Zionists. There are some religious people who also study at our school, but it is not a religious school." L. seems to believe that the school has a role to play in strengthening the Jewish identity of the second and third generation of local Jews whose connection to Judaism has weakened, compared with their ancestors:

> My generation, [. . .] second generation to the Holocaust, have already experienced economic success here. They were interested in Jewish issues but to a lesser degree than their parents. Their children or grandchildren we meet today at school, the challenge is to be with them and try to educate them in light of Jewish tradition.

G., an emissary teacher from Israel (at the time of the interview was 1.5 years in the city), describes the expansion of the ultra-Orthodox community and the decline of the Jewish-religious community like them. The expansion of the ultra-Orthodox stream in Antwerp makes it difficult for her to find suitable educational institutions for her children: "I think one of the experiences that surprised me, [. . .] is the decline of the religious community, [. . .] since they are constantly on the move from here elsewhere, or to a more ultra-Orthodox frameworks. Thus, educational options are very limited, and it affects my children directly and my own experience."

However, she notes with admiration the formal and informal education systems that the Jewish community in Antwerp manages to maintain, including highlighting Jewish and Zionist symbols that she says even exceed their ideological level of education in the country:

> It is very, very impressive and amazing to see how they manage to live here, and yet also provide Jewish education, and in *Tachkemoni* [the name of the Jewish school where G. teaches, L. L.] there is a very Zionist education, there are *Bnei Akiva*. It is very exciting

to see them in their heyday. They have the flag of Israel and the Hebrew language, these are things that are sometimes more Zionist as if we in Israel are able to give.

Similarly to L., G. describes a parallel pattern, whereas children drop out of school where she teaches and prefer non-Jewish schools, which she believes may lead to assimilation in the not too distant future:

Today the community is dealing with the *Tachkemoni* school. A lot of children, what once was not, go out and study outside, in the Flemish school and then all the talk begins: 'So in the next generation in this generation he will already get married with Flemish people; she will not be Jewish, the Jews will be assimilated', as if it were a concept that entered the community here, which never was, it seems to me.

6.3 From Personal Perspectives: Communal Integration and Social Networks: "I Have a Feeling That We Are Both Flying to the Same Destination, but to Two Different Destinations"

6.3.1 Integration within Jewish Local Communities: Social, Communal, Educational and Cultural

Respondents were asked to describe various aspects of their relationships and involvement with the local Jewish native-born community in the questionnaires (Table 9).[10] The total average of in-group involvement was moderate (mean=3.24; standard deviation=0.91), whereas sending their children to the same Jewish educational institutions, mutual assistance, social relations, community cohesiveness and marital ties were scored highest and in-group economic relations – the lowest. High standard deviations, particularly regarding children's education in Jewish institutions and activities as cohesive community, point to a high degree of variance among the respondents, with some reporting a large extent of such activities and some reporting none at all.

As for respondents' perceptions regarding their involvement and inter-relations with native-born Jews in their city, native-born respondents report slightly higher rates of all the variables: Economic, social, cultural and communal. However, differences were not significant, and the total average of inter-relations was moderate: 3.38 and 3.06 and similar standard deviation (0.88 among native-born and 0.90 among immigrants). In only two components

---

10 The quote in the title is from an interview with D. from Paris.

significant differences were found: Native-born Jews reported on in-group marriage to a higher extent than immigrants (mean=3.59; standard deviation=1.16 and 2.97; 1.47 accordingly), In addition, Native-born also send their children to Jewish institutions more than immigrants (mean=3.64; standard deviation=1.18 and 3.27; 1.54, respectively).

Table 9: Integration components with local Jewish community, as perceived by respondents – by city of residence. ANOVA (1= Not at all; 5= To a very large extent).

	All (N=440)	Paris (N=238)	Brussels (N=148)	Antwerp (N=54)	Significance of differences
	Mean (SD)	Mean (SD)	Mean (SD)	Mean (SD)	
Strong social relations	3.45 (1.15)	3.35 (1.17)	3.58 (1.14)	3.53 (1.05)	n.s.
Strong economic relations	2.93 (1.27)	2.91 (1.27)	2.84 (1.24)	3.32 (1.28)	n.s.
Mutual cultural activities	3.13 (1.15)	2.90^2 (1.18)	3.36^1 (1.08)	3.52^1 (1.02)	F=10.78**
Mutual leisure activities	3.10 (1.15)	2.96^2 (1.19)	$3.22^{1,2}$ (1.10)	3.41^1 (1.08)	*F=4.40
Marriage relations	3.33 (1.33)	3.58^2 (1.15)	3.14^1 (1.43)	2.83^1 (1.55)	F=9.20**
Joint children's education	3.48 (1.36)	3.24^2 (1.33)	3.77^1 (1.29)	$3.72^{1,2}$ (1.49)	F=7.67**
Mutual aid	3.45 (1.10)	3.48 (1.10)	3.38 (1.07)	3.53 (1.21)	n.s.
Donation to Jewish organizations	3.00 (1.25)	2.86^2 (1.29)	$3.06^{1,2}$ (1.19)	3.45^1 (1.16)	F=4.99**
Act as a cohesive community	3.36 (1.17)	3.48^2 (1.17)	3.14^1 (1.08)	$3.38^{1,2}$ (1.35)	F=3.82*
Index of integration within the non-Jewish community (Cronbach's alpha=0.89)	3.24 (0.90)	—	—	—	n.s.

*05 or less; **.01 or less; n.s.=not significant.

When compared by city of residence, there were four significant differences (Table 9) 1) Mutual cultural activities with native-born Jews were much more prevalent among the residents of Antwerp and Brussels than among those living in Paris; 2) Marriages with native-born Jews were more prevalent among the residents of Paris than among those living in Brussels and Antwerp; 3) Sending their children to the city's Jewish educational institutions was more common among the residents of Brussels and Antwerp than among those living in Paris; and 4) Contributions to the city's Jewish institutions were more prevalent among the residents of Antwerp, whereas Brussels and Paris residents tend to donate to lower degrees.

When analyzing the impact of more background variables, such as gender, age and ethnic origin (*Sephardi* or *Ashkenazi*), the most influential variable is nativity: Native-born are more integrated in the local Jewish community, compared with immigrants. In addition, younger generation (16–49 years old) feel more integrated, as do *Sephardi*, compared with older respondents (50+), from *Ashkenazi* ethnic origin. As for city of residence, those from Belgian cities, particularly Antwerp, feel more integrated in the local Jewish community.

Furthermore, as for formal and informal Jewish education items were included at the questionnaires: Studying in Jewish day school and participation in Jewish-Zionist youth movement. The average degree of youth movement participation is 3.20 (standard deviation=1.66), whereas studying in Jewish day school is slightly higher (mean=3.60, standard deviation=1.68). When compared between native-born and immigrants there is only one significant difference: Native-born send their children to Jewish day school to higher degree than immigrants. In addition, the first group is more homogeneous than the second in this context. (mean=3.72, standard deviation=1.58; mean=3.46, standard deviation=1.80).

These two educational components are different by city of residence. The respondents' children seem to participate in Jewish educational activities, to a larger degree in the Belgian cities, compared with those from Paris. Brussels is 'strongest' regarding informal activities, whereas both Belgian cities have solid formal Jewish day schools (Table 10).

Four interviewees described their own relationship and involvement with the local Jewish community: The first two are husband and wife, native-born residing in Paris, the other two are a long-term immigrant from Israel to Paris and the fourth is a native-born who reside in Brussels.

I. from Paris, pointed to the difficulties she experiences in her local Jewish community due to the fact that their children are married to non-Jews. Although she and her husband are constantly bother with questions regarding her children, they do come on holidays:

Table 10: Educational activities by city of residence – ANOVA (1= Not at all; 5= To a very large extent).

	All N=401 Mean (SD)	Paris N=208 Mean (SD)	Brussels N=140 Mean (SD)	Antwerp N=53 Mean (SD)	Significance of differences
Children participate in Jewish-Zionist youth movement	3.20 (1.66)	2.63^1 (1.57)	3.91^2 (1.44)	3.55^2 (1.74)	F=29.65**
Children study in Jewish day school	3.60 (1.68)	3.26^1 (1.80)	3.97^2 (1.39)	3.98^2 (1.65)	F=9.21**

*P<.05; **P<.01

> It's difficult for me to be very close with the community because they ask you all the time, those kinds of things, and ok, they [her children] are not married with Jews. I told them that they found a good people as spouses. They came for *Rosh Hashana* [New Year], *Kippur* [Day of Atonement], Hannuka, Purim and *Pessach*.[Passover]

O., her husband, a native-born too, elaborates regarding their feelings of exclusion from the synagogue, which was once a place where particularly his wife was involved in its activities:

> There is a synagogue not far from here [. . .], my wife was quite involved in the synagogue, we had more friends from the synagogue and more Jewish people you know. Now they are all gone, I mean from the synagogue, because it's far away [. . .] but we insisting on going to the synagogue.

D. seems to feel that the Jewish community in Paris is foreign to him and he is not attached to it. They are perceived by him as members of another ethnic group: "I see them on the plane, I have a feeling that we are both flying to the same destination, but to two different destinations. [. . .] We live in France but we are not in the same country." However, in contrast to the complete detachment that emerge from D.'s words, he also mentions some communalities with Jews in Paris:

> As soon as we sit and talk, we will laugh, we will understand each other. We have some things, especially me who is half Oriental and half European, and I have lived with Moroccans for four years, and I know some expressions, so I recognize my DNA in them and vice versa. But culturally we do not have much in common. I have much more in common with the people [non-Jews] I see on a daily basis.

F., a native-born from Brussels, is even more detached from the Jewish community in her city. She described it as consisting of 'people' and others. F.'s words imply that the group of Jews known as 'people,' is characterized by great closeness; the parents are friends with each other, their raise their children and spend holidays together and are not necessarily religious. F. does not feel connected to them and even slightly mocks their closure:

> Everything is closed. They go to school, they come home from school they do homework on the weekends, they go to a Jewish movement with those [kids] they see in school. [. . .] Then they go on vacations, they go to Israel to the beach, [. . .] to ski, where they meet in the same place. [. . .] I do not connect to them at all. [. . .] I do not understand this. This is my personal point of view.

6.3.2 Social Networks

Research participants were asked (in the questionnaires) to describe their social networks: Whether they have close friends from several ethnic groups. More than half the respondents (55%) indicated that among their good friends, most or all are local native-born Jews. Of the other groups, the non-Jewish immigrants were the most distant group, with only 7% indicating that people from this group are among their good friends (Table 11).

Two significant differences were found when compared between native-born and immigrants: Native-born group had more close friends among other local native-born Jews (mean=3.65, standard deviation=0.95) than did the immigrants (mean=3.08, standard deviation=0.94), while immigrants have more close friends among other immigrant Jews, namely diasporic group (mean=2.32, standard deviation=1.04) than do those in the native-born group (mean=2.11, standard deviation=0.99). Thus, native-born are more prone to in-group community attachment compared with immigrants who share diasporic connections primarily.

Significant differences were found in almost all variables when compared by city of residence. Having close friend among native-born Jews is typical mainly of the residents of Paris, and similarly, though less so, of the residents of the Belgian cities. In accordance with the trends I already pointed out, a relatively moderate number of residents of Brussels indicated that their social networks also include non-Jews, thus significantly differentiating them from the residents of Paris and Antwerp, who have few social connections with non-Jewish native-born groups. There are almost no non-Jewish immigrant friends in the social networks of the three groups, though the residents of Brussels are friendlier with these immigrants than are the residents of Paris and Antwerp. With respect to Jews who live in Israel, such transnational ties are not very typical of any of the groups, though the residents of Paris have even fewer such connections than those living in the Belgian cities, particularly Antwerp (Table 11).

Table 11: Social networks – best friends (percentages) and by city (ANOVA, means and standard deviations).

	All participants (percentages; N= 455)					Paris (N=239)	Brussels (N=143)	Antwerp (N=53)	Significance of differences
	None	Some	About half	Most of them	All of them	Mean (SD)	Mean (SD)	Mean (SD)	
Local native-born Jews	3	17	25	45	10	3.58^1 (0.97)	3.21^2 (0.97)	3.18^2 (1.00)	**F=7.87
Local native-born non-Jews	18	42	26	13	1	2.28^1 (1.00)	2.58^2 (0.88)	$2.19^{1,3}$ (0.88)	**F=5.30
Other local Jewish immigrants	27	41	19	11	2	2.14 (1.04)	2.23 (0.94)	2.35 (1.11)	n.s
Local non-Jewish immigrants	52	33	8	6	1	1.59^1 (0.92)	2.02^2 (0.98)	$1.45^{1,3}$ (0.57)	**F=12.22
Jews who reside in Israel	18	47	23	9	3	2.17^1 (0.86)	$2.39^{1,2}$ (0.95)	2.62^2 (1.19)	*F=6.03*

*P<.05; **P<.01; n.s.=not significant

A mixture of interviewees, immigrants (7) and native-born (7) describe their social networks and their structure: Those who are their 'best friends.' This section as the previous one will be divided according to city of residence.

6.3.2.1 Paris

As for social networks and their structure, Rabbi M. did not elaborate much about his social networks, and even wondered about the question: "Who are your close friends?" as an immediate response to my question "Who are your best friends?" He perceives his wife as being best friend: "People you work with. 'Good friends' is a big word. My best friend is my wife. After that there are people you believe in, respect them. It's the community here I really like."

On the other hand, D. elaborated about his best friends, and even tried to define for himself what a good friend is, noting that he does not have many of those in Paris. D. was wondering though whether this friendship would last when they moved to another neighborhood. He was more confident about his friends in Israel:

> How do you know who is a good friend? A good friend is one I usually invite to eat lunch or dinner. Either I call him when I need something and I do not apologize for calling him just because I need something. So, I do not have many such friends. The real friends are in Israel. [. . .] The Jews I know [. . .] their identity as Jews varies from one to another: There are those who live in total denial, and there are those for whom identity is a completely a cultural matter and they are fighting to preserve it. I have Israeli friends here, who I know most of them from before the time I came here. I know some who have been here for many years and left, and I somehow miss them.

Hence, D.'s social ties in Paris are multicultural, but temporary and superficial. From D.'s words, it seems that despite the years that have passed since his emigration to France [the eighties], the real friends by his definition are Israelis in Israel and the few with whom he was or still is in contact today:

R. and N., a married couple both born in France, mentioned social networks based mainly on Jewish friends and their family members: "[Most of the friends] are Jews. We also meet a lot with our families. We are very attached to our families." They mention their neighbor, a French Catholic, with whom they have a certain connection. However, their words imply that their ties with non-Jews are very loose: "For example, on Purim, we knock on her door we tell her to come. She is Catholic, very religious, Interested in the Jewish religion. She asks us many questions about religion."

O., a native of France, described the Jewish social networks in which his wife had previously been involved through her activities in the neighborhood synagogue. Over the years these friends have left: "There is a synagogue not far from here, and so, during that period of time, she [his wife] was quite involved in the synagogue. We had more friends from the synagogue and more Jewish people friends. Now they are all gone, I mean from the synagogue, because it's far away but we insist on going there."

O. and his wife, I. noted that their friends now are mostly Jews, from I.'s past work. O. claims that most of their friends are French (probably non-Jews): "The other friends are from my work in the past. The other one was catholic, French" and O. adds, "A lot of them are French."

6.3.2.2 Brussels and Antwerp

Rabbi A., an immigrant residing in Brussels, describes social networks in which he is involved in as superficial and casual – through his work mainly: "In Brussels it's circumstantial people that I work with, and people that I met in institutions that we meet often and we talk." He notes that his friends are scattered all over the world and that overall, he feels lonely in Brussels despite his acquaintance with many people but they are not his friends:

> Basic friends I have many in Brussels, and a lot from my youth, from the Yeshiva, they are scattered around the world, Argentina, America, Israel, you know, everywhere. I'm a bit lonely here, in friendship I can have a conversation with 100 people in Brussels, I know many people, but friends?

A., a resident of Brussels and a native of Belgium, described a process of distancing himself from his Jewish roots, partially by having social ties with non-Jews, at university and in general. After he married and had children, he distanced himself a little from his non-Jewish friends and together with his family returned to Jewish networks:

> For years, I didn't have any Jewish contacts. Of course, I have very good friends from school still, because I went to a Jewish school, which means I was with the same people from age two until eighteen: Same school, same people, exactly the same. That is why I would say I developed friendships that are still valid, active today with non-Jewish people, so I see that even though we know many non-Jewish people in very good terms, friends, or former friends that we don't see so much anymore, it is today very much focused on the Jewish world, socially.

F. from Brussels, a native born as well, noted that her best friends are mostly non-Jews. She says that Jews are too 'closed':

> These are not people from the Jewish environment at all [. . .]. One of my best friends is a Jew. But I get upset by this 'Judaism'. [. . .] Sometimes he is not an open person like me. [. . .] It does not prevent us from being friends. But my friends are not from the Jewish environment   (*milieu*, originally in French).

J., a long-term immigrant who resides in Antwerp, describes very mixed and transnational social networks: "My friends are mixed, they really are. The people that say, that I would really trust are Jewish and non-Jewish. I have really good friends. I think that Jewish friends are people that I have made more in other countries than here. It's very mixed."

Y., who immigrated to Antwerp following a marriage from Israel (to which she emigrated from Libya at the age of 14) describes a mixed social network, consisting of mostly conservative Jews and non-Jews. She particularly noted a close Christian-Protestant society and thus is exceptional in relation to the other interviewees who described more closed-Jewish networks and a minority of significant connections with locals, veterans, and non-Jews. To my question "Who are your best friends?" Y. replied: "Ah . . . both Jews and non-Jews. Of course, Jews but those who keep *Kosher*, some keep *Shabbat*. I have non-Jewish friends who are very good. I have a Protestant friend from the day I came here. We are very good friends, we raised the children together. [. . .] She's a native born." Y. later noted that it is easy for her to connect with "Gentiles" as well, although not with Muslims: "I connect really quickly. It is true that I do not, have Muslim friends."

M., an immigrant from Israel, describes social-ethnic networks of Israelis like him that are dwindling due to their return to Israel and some locals – probably Jews (since he says they do *Shabbat* together) – with whom they communicate in French and English:

> Some are Israelis, religious group, who came here many years ago. A large part of them have already left. [. . .] And we also have a group of another, four or five couples who are from here. Speak French, English. In total we have about ten families of friends, with whom we are hosted, [or] they are hosted with us.

G., an emissary teacher from Israel living in Antwerp for a year and a half, notes that they have few friends among the Jewish and Israeli emissaries. Instead, she connects with the school principal who is not Jewish. G. expresses feelings of loneliness:

> There are the emissaries of *Bnei Akiva*, who are usually younger, but they are not families. We have no friends, we have no one to go out with in the evening and such. On the other hand, we have friends as if from the community, from those who work with us, so yes Christians. Last year the principal, we were in very good relations with her and her husband. [. . .] I must say it is not as we thought it would be, I mean the feeling of loneliness.

C., although a native-born residing in Antwerp, describes his social life as meager: "So, I live my life, I go to work, sometimes I would travel abroad, a lot in

South Africa and everything and I come home and I have no social life, we have some friends in Brussels but some made Aliyah."

6.4 Summary

Not all interviewees could offer a macro picture of the Jewish local structure, but from those who did it, both immigrants (primarily long-term) and native-born, it seems that the three communities are perceived as vivid and as constantly changing. However, there are some differences among the three. While the Parisian community is the largest, and thus offer numerous Jewish community services, the Belgian communities are much smaller and less homogenous in their characteristics.

Furthermore, the Parisian community went through dramatic change in its demographic structure, whereas Ashkenazi Jews who constituted the majority there are aging, and North Africans, who immigrated mainly during the fifties through the seventies – *Sephardi* Jews, took their positions in almost all components and gave the community a more traditional and less liberal-secular character. *Ashkenazi* Jews and their children are more prone to assimilation and although they are financially well-off, they tend to donate to Israel rather than be involved in the Jewish community. Thus, their position in the Jewish community in Paris became marginal. Although some of them have being involved in the past, in a liberal-religious way, *Ashkenazi* participants hardly come to the local synagogue.

As for respondents' perceptions regarding their own integration with local Jewish community, naturally native-born are more involved economically, socially, culturally and communally, due to their nativity. Interestingly, younger respondents, as well as *Sephardi* feel more involved as well. Since *Sephardi* reside mainly in Paris, probably the younger generation there is more attached to the local community, unlike their parents, as was found regarding this cohort in other studies (see, for example, Graham, 2018). Interviewees in Paris, from *Ashkenazi* origin and older than fifty, emphasize their detachment and even exclusion from the local Jewish community, which once was very important to them, including its organizations. Belgian residents reported on their involvement and integration in the local Jewish communities by sending their children to Jewish day schools, particularly in Antwerp, and to informal Jewish and Zionist educational organizations in Brussels – although not religious.

Regarding social networks, immigrant respondents seem to have more transnational and diasporic connections (particularly with Israel), regardless of the years they reside in the city. Some also mentioned friends from work. The few native-born who responded to this question of 'close friends' either have very few, or mention Jewish friends and family as their close friends. Some refer to being left alone after their friends emigrated from the country. There are some interviewees who described their social networks as comprised from local non-Jewish friends as well – both immigrants and native-born. The quantitative results regarding social networks and their structure reveals that each group – immigrants and native-born – have social ties mainly among themselves and few have out-group friends, particularly non-Jews. From their words in the interviews as well as in the questionnaires, it implies that in the three cities there are those who feel isolated versus others who are more integrated or even tend to social assimilation. Parisians tend more toward ethno-social segregation than do those in Jews in Belgian cities, particularly in Brussels, who have higher tendency towards assimilation. Those residing in Antwerp, some themselves immigrants (particularly Israelis), have in-group social networks, similar to those from Paris but with more emphasis on transnational networks – with friends and family in Israel.

Structure, involvement and social networks, although have some similarities, differ when compared between native-born and immigrants in the three cities, whereas city of residence seems to be more important in explaining these components. Each Jewish community is unique in its structure, vitality and inter-relations. In the next and last chapter, I will present further qualitative and quantitative data which will focus on perceptions, attitudes and feelings regarding ethnic identity and identification. These findings will elaborate and deepen previous findings comparing native-born and immigrants, residing in the three cities.

Chapter 7
Ethnic Identity and Identification: Challenges, Continuity and Revival

7.1 Overview

In this chapter I will focus on ethnic identity and identification among participants. This chapter will present both quantitative and qualitative analyses which will point out differences in patterns of ethnic identity and identification among the study participants comparing among three cities, as well as between immigrants and native-born.

As mentioned in the theoretical introduction to this book, ethnic identity is defined as beliefs, values and feelings toward an ethnic group (Rebhun, 2001; Lev Ari, 2013): It is constructed dynamically and continues to develop following changes in the location of the group and the individual and changes according to the social structure of the destination nation or community (Lev Ari, 2013). Ethnic identification is the outer and behavioral expression of identity, and its components are manifested through expression of opinions and viewpoints and through actual behavior linking the individual to a particular ethnic group (DellaPergola, 2011a).

7.1.1 Cultural integration, ethnic identity and identification in France

Jews in France who emigrated from the Maghreb countries between the fifties to the seventies, had strong links to the former colonial regimes and attachment to Israel. Due to the new political and social order, Maghreb Jews decided to emigrate from their countries of origin (Abitbol and Astro, 1994). In addition, Algerian Jews in France (mainly those residing in Paris), who constitute the majority of Maghreb Jews in France, are unique in having some transnational cultural and ethnical attachment to Algeria, due to its exclusionary citizenship laws (Cohen E. H., 2009; Everett, 2017).

French Jewry present themselves as traditional and as having strong ties to Israel, manifested, for example, in their many trips to Israel (Cohen E. H., 2009). This affinity grew stronger during the Six Day War; prior to the war Israel was a cause for concern among French Jews, and after Israel's victory, French Jews tended to identify with Israel (Dahan, 2015).

https://doi.org/10.1515/9783110698817-007

Many French Jews are either secular or traditional. The major organized religious denomination in France is modern orthodoxy. An estimated seven percent of French Jews are ultra-Orthodox, and an estimated five percent are either Conservative or Reform (World Jewish Congress, 2020).

The majority of French Jews (80%) were born to both parents who are Jewish, 7% have only a Jewish father, 7% have only a Jewish mother and 6% were born to non-Jewish parents. It seems that 85%-87% are Jews by birth (see also secondary analysis of the FRA 2018 data of 3894 French Jews). The rates of intermarriage are relatively low 22%), compared with other West European countries, such as Germany and Sweden (38% in each) (DellaPergola and Staetsky, 2020; Graham, 2018).

A comparison of eight European nations found that in France, where Jews expressed the strongest feelings of being part of the Jewish people, they also have the strongest level of emotional attachment to Israel. Seventy percent of French Jews consider supporting Israel as a very important component of their Jewish identity, and 75% visited Israel but did not live there (Graham, 2018). The French result is surprising since, theoretically, the Republic 'demands' loyalty to the French state alone, and French-Jewish identification with a second state (e.g. Israel) could be construed as dual loyalty and thus controversial. However, another survey confirms the finding that 'the Jews of France in general have strong ties to Israel' (Cohen E. H., 2009, 124–125).

Regarding the sense of Jewish peoplehood, based on scores of 'Very important,' the feeling is strongest in France at 82%, and weakest in Italy (46%) (Trigano, 2007, 3). Officially, Jewish peoplehood in France is not supposed to exist. With regard to Jewish practice (ethnic identification), France stands out compared with other western countries: A relatively high proportion (20%), (second among eight European counties), follows five or six religious practices (Attend *Seder* [Passover meal], keep the *Shabbat*, eat only *Kosher* meat at home, attend synagogue weekly or more often, light candles most Friday nights, fast on *Yom Kippur* most or all years), compared with the proportion (26%) that follows one or no practice (Graham, 2018).

When asked about the sense of attachment to the Jewish people and to their current country of residence, 96% have strong feelings towards the first group while 83% are attached to France. The integration model according to Berry (see also in Lev Ari and Cohen N., 2018) – i.e. feeling a sense of closeness to both the Jewish people and general society – is the most prevalent in France, as well as in Sweden and in the UK (Graham, 2018).

Jewish practice of French Jews differs by age and ethnic origin, among other factors. For example, Jewish practice is less intense among those who are older (65+ years old), compared with young people (35 or less); 18% and 53%

practice Jewish religion, respectively. The rest in each group do not practice re-ligion. Furthermore, celebrating Jewish high holidays is more frequent among *Sephardi*, compared with *Ashkenazi*: Among those who celebrate *Yom Kippur* (53% of the total sample), 74% of *Sephardi* and only 45% of *Ashkenazi* observe this High Holiday. The same pattern appears regarding Passover (51% of the total sample celebrate); 65% of *Sephardi* and 48% of *Ashkenazi* celebrate this High Holiday. Forty nine percent celebrate *Rosh Hashana*; 65% *Sephardi* and 45% *Ashkenazi* (Fourquet, 2015). Only a third of (36%) of Jews in France re-ported that religion is the main factor in defining their Jewish identity (Della-Pergola and Staetsky, 2020).

7.1.2 Cultural integration, ethnic identity and identification in Belgium

Two thirds of Belgian Jews (68%) were born to both parents who are Jewish; 14% have only a Jewish father, 9% have only a Jewish mother and 10% were born to non-Jewish parents. Thus, 77% are Jewish by birth while a third are not – according to Jewish Halacha [law]. Rates of intermarriage among Belgian Jews are relatively low (20%) (DellaPergola and Staetsky, 2020; Graham, 2018). In another data, based on 786 Jewish respondents, 90% described themselves as "Jewish by birth," 8% converted, and the others are not Jewish (secondary analysis of the FRA, 2018).

With respect to identity and ethnic identification among Jews of Belgium, 40% consider themselves secular Jews, 15% define themselves liberal, more than a quarter see themselves traditional, and a sixth define themselves Ortho-dox. Moreover, the Jewish community in Belgium is strong and pluralistic, and its character emerges in an excellent school system alongside cultural compo-nents such as the press, the radio, synagogues and clubs that provide Belgian Jews with tools to cope with antisemitism (Ben-Rafael, 2017). Similarly to Jews in France, slightly more than a third (38%) reported that religion is the main factor in defining their Jewish identity (DellaPergola and Staetsky, 2020).

When asked about their feelings of attachment to the Jewish people and to their current country of residence, 93% have strong feelings towards the first group while 63% are attached to Belgium. Sixty percent of Belgian Jews con-sider supporting Israel as a very important component of their Jewish identity, and 71% visited Israel but did not live there (Graham, 2018).

As for Jewish practice (ethnic identification), a relatively high proportion (18%) follows five or six religious' practices, compared with 29% that follows one or no practice; they are the fourth among eight European counties, This may reflect religious segmentation within the country.

Regarding Berry's acculturation model (see also Lev Ari and Cohen N., 2018), the separation/segregation strategy is the second most prevalent (after integration), i.e. a feeling of closeness to the Jewish people but greater distance from the broader local society, and this is most prevalent in Germany and in Latvia and to a lesser extent, in Belgium (Graham, 2018).

7.2 Jewish Background: A Comparison by Cities of Residence and Groups (Native-Born and Immigrants)

Since this study was aimed at Jewish participants, almost all of them (94%) were born as such (the rest were either converted to Judaism or not religiously affiliated). When compared by groups, native-born versus immigrants, there are no significant differences regarding respondents' Jewishness and that of their parents and spouses. However, it should be noted that among native-born and immigrants less than a tenth were not born as Jewish (10% and 7%, respectively). As for their current spouses, there are some rates of intermarriage, in both groups: 13% among native-born, and 18% among immigrants.

Comparing by city of residence, there are some significant differences. In Paris and Antwerp 96% of the participants were born Jewish, compared with 91% in Brussels. Although this difference is not that large, the participants' mothers are mostly Jewish among those in Paris and Antwerp (95%), while in Brussels only 84% were born as Jewish (5% converted and another 11% are not Jewish or religiously affiliated). Regarding fathers' Jewish origin, there is no significant difference. As for their spouses, 96% of those in Antwerp, 89% in Paris and 71% in Brussels are Jewish.

Thus, when Jewish background is studied city of residence is more significant; this might affect further results, particularly regarding ethnic identity and identification, to be demonstrated in this chapter.

7.3 Jewish Ethnic Identity

In this section I will focus on three dimensions of ethnic identity: Inner attitudes and feelings toward an ethnic group, transnational with regard to country of origin and particularly to Israel and its various implications on ethnic identity as well as multiple, or hyphenated identities and thus, inherent conflicts of identities.

7.3.1 Transnational Identity and Attachment to Israel: "I Am Totally at 'Home' in the Two Countries"

Part of ethnic identity could be associated with feelings of belonging to a country or city, namely feeling 'at home'; Israel, in particular, has a central and special place not only as part of a transnational ethnic identity, but also in itself, and not only for those who were born in it.[11]

7.3.1.1 Paris

The first three interviewees from Paris are long-term immigrants from Israel. The sense of ambivalence in his status as former immigrant and his strong attachment to Israel, versus France, is prominent in Rabbi M.'s words: "Even now, when I have been here for seventeen years, I'm not really here. [. . .] I still feel like I'm on a trip." Rabbi M. elaborates regarding his transnational identity: "I learned a lot to love the culture, the people. The family, my children were born here, my wife [was born] here, so there is 'home' here. [. . .] I grew up in Israel, my childhood and all that. But, sure it's our home, but I feel like it's my home here, too, very different homes though."

D., another long-term immigrant from Israel as well, says: "I am totally 'at home' in the two countries, I am completely split." To my question: "Between which places?" He replied: "Between Tel Aviv and Paris." That is a transnational sense of home in two urban geographical spaces – this often characterizes immigrants.

H., also a former immigrant from Israel, defines herself as a 'guest' and eternal stranger who does not feel affiliated with any country, but feels 'at home' in Paris, although seems to have positive feelings towards the Kibbutz in Israel. She describes a deliberate maintenance of being a stranger over the years:

> I did not come as an immigrant. [. . .] I just stayed. [. . .] I take myself as a guest and this situation for me is wonderful. I love being a stranger. I am also a stranger in Israel. [. . .] I adopt the things I love. I will never be French. [. . .] I feel 'at home' where I feel good. [. . .] Today I have a feeling that Israel went a different way, and I went a different way. I feel 'at home' here. In Israel I come for a week or two, I feel good because I have friends, I can go to the Kibbutz, which I love very much. I do not spit into the well, on the contrary, I drink from it.

The next two interviewees are long-term immigrants from Morocco, who came in their teens to France. Rabbi Y. describes feelings of 'home' in his country of

---

11 The quote in the title is from an interview with D. from Paris.

origin which he left at a young age (12 years): "Last year I was in Morocco, for Rabbi Shimon Bar Yochai's celebration. I really was 'at home.' That is how it was, we would go to the same place with the parents and the family, so we remembered everything."

Rabbi Y., also seems to have a significant connection to Israel. The rabbi's wife has been educated in a Jewish-Zionist school and most of their children live in Israel:

> The first time I came here to *Eretz Israel* [the land of Israel], it was in honor of my *Bar Mitzvah* [Jewish coming of age ritual]. [. . .] I was young, thirteen years old. [. . .] As a rabbi, I supported Israel a lot, which is not just a state, but the Jewish people should live there. [. . .] My wife is very Zionist. She attended a school called *Yavneh* in Marseille which was Zionist. [. . .] She insisted that our sons would love the Land of Israel so much that today six out of our seven children are here in Jerusalem.

S. does not feel like an immigrant at all: "Someone who has lived here for forty-fifty years does not feel like an immigrant. It feels as Jews but not as immigrants." He feels more 'at home' in France than previous interviewees and makes a distinction between the more material aspect identified with France and the spiritual-Jewish aspect identified with Israel, as kind of 'imagined community.' S. mentions Israel's central place since his childhood in Morocco and as part of his school curriculum there:

> When I was a child [. . .], at home in Morocco, I remember my mother sitting at the radio to listen to news from Israel. She also listened to the Voice of America in foreign languages, but Israel was very central. Religious life was around Israel, in school we learned about it and I even had teachers who came from Israel.

The last three interviewees are native-born of France. N. and R., a married couple, whom I interviewed together, indicate different feelings of 'home': While N. notes that she felt good in Israel but understood that living there would make it difficult for her professionally and familywise, R. expresses less enthusiasm regarding Israel and feels more 'at home' in Paris. N.: "In Israel, I feel good. When I am there, I tell myself that I would like to live there. Even though I know that professionally it is difficult. And leaving my family is difficult," and R. notes that: "When I travel for vacation to Israel, I am very happy to go there but not to live there. I am happy to return here, to my place."

O., another native of France, describes a sense of 'home' in Paris but also in Israel: "I feel 'at home' here. All those years after I came back [from Israel], I was feeling at 'home' in Israel as well."

7.3.1.2 Brussels

Five interviews from Brussels were analyzed: Two immigrants, one from Israel and another from Argentina, and three native-born. B., an Israeli who immigrated to Brussels at a relatively older age (forties), followed her dream to reside in her mother's country of origin. Her sense of 'home' in Brussels is particularly strong for an immigrant:

> I feel here 'at home'. I am a stranger but 'at home.' [. . .] I have my sports club, two or three closest friends. Although my best friends are in Israel, I do feel 'at home' here. When I travel to Israel, [. . .] I say to myself that it is a good feeling knowing that in three weeks I will be back here.

B. also describes having transnational ties with her son, and emphasizes that there might be two houses, which makes it easier for her to stay in Brussels: "I sit with my son and talk to him on weekends for an hour, two hours on Facebook and we see each other and talk. It is not what used to be thirty years ago [. . .]. I have two houses, why do you need only one house?"

Habad rabbi A., who was born in Argentina, feels a stranger, compared with his wife and children who are French-Canadian. Israel seems to be the most significant country, as far of his Jewish-religious identity is concerned:

> Yes, definitely [I feel as an immigrant], my wife is French, and my kids are French. The benefit of this area is that all are immigrants. So constantly we are surrounded, we are at a *Shabbat* table [we share the same table] with Jews from Germany, France, the UK, Slovakia, from everywhere, so it feels alright, we are not weird people from the world. [. . .]. Today, I probably [feel 'at home'] nowhere. Because if I go back to Argentina, at first, I'd love it. Afterwards, there are certain things that I am not used to, because I'm outside of Argentina some 17 years [. . .] The State of Israel is the number one country that I have more links to, because of our history.

A., a native-born of Belgium, describes a very ambivalent sense of 'home.' He describes a weak sense of transnational identity, which does not make him uncomfortable: "I do not fully belong anywhere, not fully in Belgium, not much in Israel, I must admit. And so, it is kind of a bit of a status, in-between limbo status, which personally I don't have a problem with." As for his attachment to Israel, it seems moderate: "Economically nothing. Socially very much, because there is a lot of family [. . .] I think I have a strong bond. I do not want to live there, but I have a strong bond which probably developed when I lived there for one year."

M., a native-born also, did not mention Belgium as his home, as expected, and described feelings of transnational belonging with emphasis on Israel: "[. . .] I will say the real place when you can be yourself 'at home,' is Israel."

F., another native-born of Belgium, described a slightly vaguer connection to Israel, but it seems to be the strongest pole in her moderate Jewish identity.

I think that in my head I am a true Jew but not at all religious because I do not believe in God. I do not celebrate the Holidays, I do not eat *Kosher* [. . .]. But in contrast, I feel some connection to Judaism, which I cannot explain. When I go to Israel for example, with the children or alone, [. . .] there is something inside me that is bubbling but I cannot put words to it.

7.3.1.3 Antwerp

Three Israeli immigrants, one British, and one native-born describe their feelings of 'home' and sense of identification with different countries. L., an Israeli immigrant, does not explicitly state the name of Israel regarding 'home,' even though he grew up there and his family and most of his friends reside there: "Where the whole family is, where my culture is, where the friends are. Where I grew up, where I see my future. This is 'home.'" However, L. seems to have a strong connection to Israel, as part of his identity and even describes the country in terms of 'womb':

> For me, the state of Israel is my identity, it is my country. I am currently living outside the womb. [. . .] Right now, we are living in our unnatural place. In all respects. Perhaps only the economic parameter and the emissary parameter can justify our stay here. Without one of these two parameters, we would not stay here even one day.

G., another short-term Israeli immigrant (one year and a half), is hesitant about 'feeling at home,' and defines it on two levels: On the concrete level of habituation and a sense of 'home,' and regarding the state level. She also describes the hardship of integration into the new place:

> It's an initial experience for me, not to be in Israel for so long. It was very difficult at first. Really, it took us almost a year and a half to adjust. Today, maybe you are more familiar, more professionally connected. You feel more comfortable. At the same time, there are a lot of things that are very different, [. . .] and you feel that you are not in your natural place. [. . .] In Israel, I really love Jerusalem [. . .]. So, Jerusalem for me is the place.

Y., who immigrated to Israel as a 14-year-old teen from Tripoli in Libya, and at the age of 26 married a Belgian and followed him to Antwerp, describes feelings of longing for Israel and especially for the family. This is a case of double migration at relatively late ages, which perhaps explains the feeling of disconnection from Israel in favor of Belgium: "At first, I cried a lot because my parents were still alive, and I really missed Israel, but today I feel 'at home' here. My children live here, my grandchildren live here, my job is here, I built a life for myself. [. . .] Now, when I come to Israel I really feel like a guest."

J., who emigrated from England many years ago, feels 'at home' in the city, but her identity is nationally divided. However, she seems to feel comfortable with her split identity: "I feel very much 'at home' here. I cannot say I feel

Belgian, but I do not feel British, either. I do not feel belonging to any country, but I feel incredibly comfortable with that. It is not a discomfort for me."

J. also refers to her attachment to Israel. She is mostly connected to certain people she knows there and not necessarily from a Jewish aspect. She points out that she may immigrate to Israel in the future, but this is not a major goal in her life. It is implied that Israel's place in her life now is not very central: "I've never had any desire to live in Israel. Doesn't mean that I wouldn't one day. When I go there, I go to visit people. I don't go there because it's Israel and I'm attached to it, but due to many people I know there."

C., who was born in Belgium describes a feeling of detachment, even though he is local: "I live here, but if I am thrown out, then I will go to another country."

7.3.2 Multiple Ethnic Identities

Ethnic identity was quantitatively analyzed, regarding Jewish ethnic identity, attachment to Israel, country of origin (for immigrants) and national-local country of residence. When comparing between native-born and immigrants, two components were found to be significant (summary indexes only): National-local identity, where native born reported having stronger attachment to current country of residence, compared with immigrants (mean=3.63, standard deviation=1.05; mean=3.16, standard deviation=0.99, respectively), and feeling as minority: Native-born also felt as a minority to a higher degree than immigrants (mean=3.30, standard deviation=1.02; mean=3.00, standard deviation=1.04, respectively).

Differences according to city of residence were found on all summary measures and almost in all variables. On the first measure, which describes emotional identity towards Judaism and Israel, those from Paris have the strongest feelings, followed by residents of Antwerp, who reported slightly lower total attachment, and then by those in Brussels, who seem to have the weakest feelings (although rather strong).

The second measure refers to feelings of attachment to and identity with participants' country of origin (Israel or other). The summary measure is lower than the previous measure (medium extent), mainly among residents of the Belgian cities, of whom a large portion are Israeli immigrants. With respect to national identity towards current country of residence, these feelings are similar to attachment to country of origin; residents of Paris emerge highest on this measure, followed by residents of Brussels and those of Antwerp, who expressed a lower level of national identity. Finally, the measure of feeling like a minority in their country of residence, is the lowest among the four summary measures, but is much stronger among Paris and Brussels residents, and lowest among those from Antwerp. Thus, in each of the four identity trajectories different feelings are reported when the three cities' residents are compared. As a whole, Jewish identity and attachment to Israel are the strongest, transnational identity with country of origin is rather strong, whereas national identity and feelings as minorities are moderate (Table 12).

When analyzing the impact of more background variables, such as gender, age, and ethnic origin (*Sephardi* or *Ashkenazi*), the most influential variable is ethnic origin; *Sephardi* have the strongest Jewish identity and attachment to Israel, compared with *Ashkenazi*; those from Paris and Antwerp more than those from Brussels; older participants more than the younger generation and native-born more than immigrants. Gender has no impact in this context.

Ethnic identity regarding country of origin is more prevalent among younger participants and those from Belgian cities, where Israeli immigrants reside mostly. Gender and ethnic origin do not influence participants' sense of identity towards country of origin. National identity characterizes native-born more than immigrants and those from Paris, compared with the Belgian cities. Age, gender and ethnic origin do not impact national identity. Finally, ethnic identity as minorities is more prevalent among those from Paris and Brussels and less among those from Antwerp, and more among men, compared to women. Age, ethnic origin, native-born versus immigrants have no affect regarding ethnic identity as minorities. Thus, city of residence is the most influential variable regarding ethnic identity, whereas other components, such as nativity versus being an immigrant, age and ethnic origin serve as additional factors with regard to components of ethnic identity.

7.3.3 Identity Conflicts: "It Turns Out That It Is Not So Easy to Escape from Identity"

In the interviews, participants were asked to refer to their ethnic identity.[12] It seems that all have multiple identities: Some, primarily immigrants, refer to their country of origin and others emphasize local-national identity, as well as Jewish identity.

D., a long-term immigrant from Israel to Paris, describes the conflict between two identities: Jewish and Israeli. He notes that he tried to escape from both, especially from the Israeli one: "In order to shake off all kinds of brainwashing that sometimes oppresses me." He well describes the difficulty in escaping from ethnic identity:

> It turns out that it is not so easy to escape from identity. If you do it you should run fast, because if identity catches you, then it 'punishes' you for trying to escape. That's what

---

12 The quote in the title is from an interview with D. from Paris.

> happened to me with both. Let's say with Jewish identity it was more difficult for me, be-cause suddenly I had to deal with all kinds of questions that were asked of me. [. . .] I have gone through some stages of my faith, although I do not practice religion, but I have been fasting for maybe twenty years on *Yom Kippur*. I was fasting and not going to syna-gogue, then I started going to synagogue, [. . .] with the tendency to see as many Jews as possible. [. . .] But I cannot say that I am a religious person, but I leave an open door here.

Regarding Israel's place in his life, D. notes the great importance he attaches to Israel, the need to feel continuity, since he emigrated from it (25 years), to meet family and friends. On the other hand, he seems to have a lot of anger towards Israeli culture:

> Whenever I have time, I travel to Israel. I 'charge the battery.' [. . .] I am a person who lives in two places. [. . .] A French person goes on vacation to a different place every time. Dis-covers all sorts of things: Once he goes to Club Med in Tunisia, once he goes to the Domini-can Republic, [. . .] but when I go to Tel Aviv, I go back home, where I was born, I meet my childhood friends, I go to the sea, I continue what I left behind in the previous round. At the same time, I have a lot of anger towards the country. I can't stand Israeli bestiality, I can't stand this direct invasive intrusion, that each allows himself to preach morality to the other, and opacity [. . .] that sometimes makes me sick, [. . .] that is close to hatred.

M. refers, first and foremost, without being asked about, and despite being born in Belgium, to the origin of his parents who were born outside of Belgium. He defines himself as *Sephardi*-Italian-Jewish: "On my father's side they immi-grated to the Belgian Congo. And on my mother's side they immigrated to Africa, to Rhodesia, English colony. So, my roots are Italian, and today I still have an Italian passport. [. . .] I define myself also as Jewish-*Sephardi*."

Y. from Antwerp, who immigrated in her twenties following marriage to her Belgian husband, describes a split identity: Belgian and Israeli. She is involved in current affairs, and follows what is happening in Israel. However, the first identity she mentions is Belgian. "I'm Belgian, but I also feel Israeli. I follow the news all the time. If something happens in the country, it hurts me as if it happened to me."

7.4 Jewish Ethnic Identification

Ethnic identification is the outer and behavioral expression of identity, linking the individual to a particular ethnic group. In this section I will present quantitative and qualitative analyses regarding three components of Jewish ethnic identification: Jewish practice, language usage and children's Jewish socialization and education.

7.4.1 Jewish Practice

In the questionnaires, respondents were asked to describe the level at which they practice Jewish customs in their daily lives. The extent to which all participants practice religion is rather high (mean=3.88). The most prevalent practices are: Participating in Passover *Seder*, celebrating the Hebrew New Year, *Rosh Hashana* and fasting on *Yom Kippur* (Day of Atonement) (Table 12). When native-born and immigrants are compared, the first group keep *Kosher* to a higher degree than do immigrants (mean=3.57, standard deviation=1.56; mean=3.21, standard deviation=1.71, respectively). In addition, native-born belong to a synagogue more than immigrants do (mean=3.73, standard deviation=1.30; mean=3.42, standard deviation=1.59). As for other customs – there are no significant differences between the two groups.

Table 12: Jewish identity regarding Judaism, Israel, country of origin, local-national and ethnic minority, by city of residence – ANOVA (1= Not at all; 5= To a very large extent).

Ethnic identity components	All	Paris N=239	Brussels N=148	Antwerp N=55	Significance of differences
	Mean (SD)	Mean (SD)	Mean (SD)	Mean (SD)	
Jewish identity and Israel – attachment					
Proud to be Jewish	4.41 (0.92)	4.61[1] (0.78)	4.08[2] (0.98)	4.44[1] (1.07)	**F=15.56
Israel serves as a spiritual center to the Jewish people	4.00 (1.11)	4.28[1] (0.96)	3.59[2] (1.14)	3.81[2] (1.31)	**F=19.06
Feel Jewish	4.70 (0.67)	4.79[1] (0.53)	4.48[2] (0.90)	4.81[1] (0.52)	**F=9.61
Have a clear sense of being Jewish	4.26 (0.90)	4.37[1] (0.80)	4.02[2] (0.99)	4.40[1] (0.98)	**F=7.72
Emotional attachment to Israel	4.29 (0.97)	4.44[1] (0.80)	4.05[2] (1.13)	4.11[1,2] (1.15)	*F=7.50*
Present yourself as Jewish	4.20 (1.09)	4.45[1] (0.89)	3.80[2] (1.27)	4.05[1,2] (1.13)	**F=15.89
Summary Index (Cronbach's alpha=0.79)	4.29 (0.68)	4.49[1] (0.56)	3.96[2] (0.74)	4.28[1] (0.70)	**F=30.83

Table 12 (continued)

Ethnic identity components	All	Paris N=239	Brussels N=148	Antwerp N=55	Significance of differences
	Mean (SD)	Mean (SD)	Mean (SD)	Mean (SD)	
Ethnic identity towards country of origin					
Feel primarily as native-born of country of origin	3.45 (1.35)	3.29 (1.41)	3.61 (1.26)	3.80 (1.19)	*F=4.01
Attached to country of origin	3.36 (1.34)	3.24 (1.36)	3.59 (1.27)	3.43 (1.39)	n.s
Feel 'at home' in country of origin	3.43 (1.41)	3.18^1 (1.45)	3.80^2 (1.27)	3.93^2 (1.18)	**F=9.40
Present yourself as a native-born from country of origin	3.59 (1.29)	3.41^1 (1.30)	3.79^2 (1.35)	3.93^2 (0.96)	**F=5.24
Summary Index (Cronbach's alpha=0.84)	3.47 (1.14)	3.28^1 (1.17)	3.66^2 (1.09)	3.85^2 (0.95)	** F=8.08
National identity towards current country of residence					
Feel French/Belgian	3.41 (1.34)	3.59^1 (1.25)	3.21^2 (1.40)	3.06^2 (1.46)	**F=5.34
Feel attached to country of residence	3.32 (1.19)	3.59^1 (1.14)	3.01^2 (1.16)	2.86^2 (1.19)	**F=15.07
Feel a 'at home' in country of residence	3.55 (1.10)	3.49 (1.13)	3.59 (1.06)	3.70 (1.07)	n.s
Summary Index (Cronbach's alpha=0.82)	3.43 (1.05)	3.56 (1.04)	3.28 (1.05)	3.22 (1.02)	*F=4.16
Feelings as minority					
Feel as minority in country of residence	3.45 (1.22)	3.56^1 (1.18)	3.47^1 (1.23)	2.94^2 (1.25)	**F=5.46
Feel different in country of residence due to being Jewish	2.89 (1.18)	3.01 (1.19)	2.82 (1.16)	2.59 (1.14)	*F=3.18
Summary Index (Cronbach's alpha=0.61)	3.17 (1.04)	3.29^1 (1.02)	3.14^1 (1.03)	2.71^2 (1.05)	**F=7.28

*P<.05; **P<.01; n.s=not significant.

The overall measure for practicing Jewish customs indicates that residents of Paris practice most customs to a slightly larger extent than those in Antwerp, while in Brussels this measure is the lowest among the three cities and points to a moderate level of practicing Jewish customs. Significant differences between the three cities were mainly in the context of eating *Kosher* meat and fasting on *Yom Kippur*, customs which are quite prevalent in Paris, moderately prevalent in Antwerp less frequent in Brussels. Regarding other customs, although sometimes the two Belgian cities are similar and sometimes Antwerp resembles Paris, it is obvious that Brussels' Jewish residents generally practice religion to the lowest degree (Table 13).

Table 13: Jewish practice by city of residence – ANOVA (1= Not at all; 5= To a very large extent).

Jewish practice components	All N=441	Paris N=239	Brussels N=148	Antwerp N=55	Significance of differences
	Mean (SD)	Mean (SD)	Mean (SD)	Mean (SD)	
Lighting *Shabbat* candles	3.53 (1.53)	3.89[1] (1.38)	3.02[2] (1.58)	3.40[1,2] (1.61)	**F=15.70
Participating in Passover *Seder*	4.38 (0.90)	4.42[1,2] (0.80)	4.20[1] (1.11)	4.69[2] (0.60)	*F=6.45*
Eating *Kosher* meat	3.41 (1.63)	4.10[1] (1.24)	2.32[2] (1.52)	3.33[3] (1.82)	**F=71.61
Fasting on *Yom Kippur*	4.09 (1.30)	4.44[1] (0.89)	3.54[2] (1.58)	4.00[1,2] (1.46)	**F=23.94
Celebrating *Rosh Hashana* (Hebrew New Year)	4.35 (0.97)	4.43[1] (0.88)	4.10[2] (1.17)	4.69[1] (0.57)	**F=8.94
Belonging to a synagogue	3.60 (1.44)	3.82[1] (1.36)	3.07[2] (1.43)	4.05[1] (1.40)	**F=16.53
Index of total Jewish practice (Cronbach's alpha=0.87)	3.88 (1.05)	4.18[1] (0.92)	3.36[2] (1.07)	4.03[1] (1.03)	**F=32.22

*P<.05; **P<.01

Furthermore, when analyzing Jewish practice by other background variables, in addition to city of residence and native born versus immigrants such as age, gender, ethnic origin (*Sephardi* or *Ashkenazi* – as defined by the respondents), several effects may be noticed. The most influential variable regarding practicing religion is ethnic origin; *Sephardi* tend to practice much more than *Ashkenazi* do, those from Antwerp and Paris more than those from Brussels, and native-born more than immigrants. Gender does not affect Jewish practice; men and women are similar in that matter.

7.4.2 Language Usage

Other components of Jewish identification are expressed in respondents' answers regarding their language usage. When respondents are asked about their primary language usage with different groups such as family, friends, colleagues and media, they answer that the usage of mother tongue is mostly prevalent within the family and slightly declines when interacting with other groups or usage of media. It is interesting to note, that at work usage of local language is not common (Table 14).

Table 14: Usage of languages with different groups (percentages).

Speak with your:	Mother tongue	Local language	Other Language	Mixture of two languages	Mixture of three languages
Spouse	64	19	3	11	3
Children	67	18	2	10	3
Work colleagues	49	18	5	17	11
Friends	50	19	2	20	9
Media (newspapers, internet etc.)	48	18	2	21	11

Obviously, language usage differs when native-born and immigrants are compared. Since language usage is more relevant to cultural integration of immigrants, I present findings which compare them and native-born, and not by city of residence.

Native-born use primarily their mother tongue (75%) and local language – which is usually the same – (13%) with their spouses and children, while immigrants use their mother tongue to a lesser degree (about 50%) but to a larger extent use local language (25%). The rest use a mixture of languages.

At work, native-born use primarily their mother tongue (59%) and local language (14%), while immigrants use their mother tongue (36%) and local language (24%). The most significant difference in language usage is when they talk with their friends; native-born use their mother tongue (64%) and local language

(15%), compared with immigrants who use a mixture of languages – mother tongue (32%), local language (26%) and a mixture of two languages (23%). As for the cultural component – the media – again, native-born use their mother tongue (59%), a mixture of two languages (20%) and local language (15%), while immigrants use their mother tongue (33%), local language (24%), a mixture of two languages (21%) or even three (19%).

In order to elaborate on the above quantitative findings regarding language usage as an expression of ethnic identification, I will present the qualitative results from the interviews.

When interviewees were asked what language they mainly use, Rabbi Y. who is a long-term immigrant from Morocco to Paris, uses mainly French in most areas except for religious purposes: "Usually French is spoken at home. I read [in French] a lot, and a lot in Hebrew, the language of the Bible. At work – all in French, even when we have a conference of rabbis, we speak French."

D. relates to his accent as an obstacle to total loss of his identification as long-term immigrant from Israel, which he seems trying to conceal:

> You know I have an accent. Now if you hear me a little, then you think I am Swiss. So, if I talk more than that, then you see I am not from here, they think I am from Eastern Europe. I explain to people that I am not European at all, and I let them guess. No one knows where I am from or my identity, I am comfortable with my anonymity.

H. a long-term immigrant from Israel to Paris, mentions that as part of her ethnic identification, she needs to read books in Hebrew, compared to newspapers she reads in French: "I read newspapers in French, I do not read books in French, because I do not have the pleasure that I have when reading in Hebrew." B., an Israeli immigrant to Brussels, describes the connection to the Israeli television channel as part of essential transnational cultural consumption: "I think we are connected here to the Israeli channel, [. . .] as to an infusion."

Rabbi A. from Brussels, an immigrant born in Argentina and a *Habad* emissary in the city, describes the use of several languages as part of his self-expression and his family's transnational ethnic identification: "At work – English, and with my family, with my kids [I speak] in Spanish. With my wife – in English. So Spanish because I [want] them to keep my language. [. . .] So French from the mother, Spanish from me, English from the community."

M., a native of Belgium, residing in Brussels, is also fluent in several languages, although French is certainly the dominant language for him as his mother tongue as well as his and his family's spoken language today. He speaks English and some Flemish and Hebrew. He proceeds, saying that it is not right to isolate his children culturally and linguistically:

> I speak French 'at home.' I was raised in French, and I still speak French today, my wife too and my kids too, so we all speak French. I do speak English obviously, I speak Dutch and a little bit of Hebrew. [. . .] My mother was a native English speaker. She came to Belgium, she wanted to speak French, she did not want to isolate her own kids by [speaking] another language or another culture. My statement is that when you come to another country, you want to integrate. You don't want to keep your kids in your own culture.

F., another native of Belgium living in Brussels mentions language as a barrier between Israelis and Belgians, including Jews. She notes this when referring to relationships between teachers at the school she runs: "Israelis segregate themselves as well as do Belgians. You [Israelis] sit at the same table – it's not that we do not want you to be integrated with us, we do talk to you, but I believe language has its affect."

Y. from Antwerp, who immigrated to Israel from Libya at the age of 14, and in her twenties immigrated to Belgium, describes the use of many languages, each indicating a station in her life:

> My native family speaks Italian. With my friends I speak Italian, of course. With my family I try to speak Hebrew. Here, at school [where she works], in Flemish and Hebrew. With my Belgian friends in Flemish. With my sister I also speak French. I have friends here, I also speak French with them. And of course, if you live in Antwerp as a Jew you must learn Yiddish. There are shops that [are run by] these Jews who speak only Yiddish, and you must learn Yiddish.

The Hebrew language serves as mother tongue to Israeli immigrants and as a holy language to some religious native-born. Language usage between parents sometimes serves as a means to orientate children towards Jewish identification and attachment to Israel, which will be discussed in the next section.

7.4.3 Children's Jewish Socialization and Education

Another component of Jewish identification is expressed by Jewish socialization and education of participants' children. In Chapter 6, I presented quantitative findings regarding children's Jewish education as part of participants' attitudes regarding their integration and involvement in the local Jewish community. In this section however, I present qualitative analysis which emphasizes education and socialization of interviewees' children as part of their parents' ethnic identification.

Rabbi M. from Paris (who is a long-term immigrant from Israel) speaks with his children in French, and regrets not speaking Hebrew with them. He sends the children to a Jewish day school so that they will absorb "Jewish atmosphere. They hear prayer, celebrate Independence Day, celebrate Jerusalem Day. Learn [Jewish] holiday songs in Hebrew."

D., another long-term immigrant who resides in Paris, has a daughter from a French, non-Jewish woman, from whom he is separated now. His daughter's Jewish education is not prioritized due to her mother's affiliation, he says, but it is important for him to give her some Jewish education, even though he himself does not define himself as religious. From a young age D. tried to expose her to Jewish customs and holidays, not always successfully:

> I myself do not celebrate [Jewish] holidays, but it was important to me that she would see and know from what context she came. If she came on the day when the fourth candle of Hanukka is lit, then I would light four candles. [. . .] I once took her to a synagogue on *Yom Kippur* and it was a nightmare. As they say: 'and you tortured your souls,' and I tortured my soul more than I expected. But of course, I did not prevent her from eating. I tried to teach her Hebrew between the ages of six and seven. She had a notebook, she knew all the letters [. . .] until at about the age of seven, when she decided she no longer wanted to speak, as someone might mock her, [. . .] and recently for three or four months she has been learning Hebrew.

Rabbi Y., currently living in Paris, previously lived in another small city in France, which did not have Jewish schools. He describes difficulties in finding a suitable school for his children where they can preserve their Jewish identity and his choice of a Catholic school that was willing to consider the issue of *Shabbat* and Jewish holiday practices. Thus, despite the lack of a Jewish school there, he found a compromise that allowed at least partial observance of Jewish customs until they arrived in Paris:

> They worked on *Shabbat*, and did not want to accept our children, because we told them we would not send them on *Shabbat*. They will come on holidays, to school, but they will have a task that the teacher will give them before the holidays, or immediately after the holidays in the evening, they will go to their friends who will give them the homework.

O., a native of France residing in Paris, describes the education they gave at home to their children as Jews. It was on the basic level, as expected of an assimilated family. However, they did visit Israel frequently and O. even spoke Hebrew: "We went regularly to Israel for holidays. And I did feel very much at home, because I spoke Hebrew fluently. [. . .] Today, I must say that it's a little more complicated." All their three children are married to non-Jews and their grandchildren also have minimal Jewish education:

> We try to give them minimal knowledge about Jewish history, the bible and holidays, so they can choose to marry a Jewish girl. We try to give them the feeling of being Jewish, through our way of life and friends. Obviously, we also know that our way of living is assimilated, and so they have now the same assimilated way of living. Our grandchildren know we are Jews and we do something here, and they do something else.

F. from Brussels, a native of Belgium, describes her relative distance from Jewish religion throughout the interview. She was also married to a non-Jew. However, she was disappointed when her husband objected to holding a circumcision [*Brit*] ceremony for her son:

> My little son's father is not Jewish. It was never a problem. He accepted that he would come here to school very easily. The only thing that made me unhappy is circumcision. [. . .] His father did not want to, he thought it was barbaric [. . .]. But I wanted, more for hygiene, not religiously. He is not circumcised but he is Jewish anyway because his mother is Jewish. Feeling Jewish, I think, like me. No more no less. He attended school here [Jewish school] until last year.

She further adds how important it is that her only son be connected to his Jewish roots, even though she is secular: "It was important because I received Jewish values from my family, from my parents, from my grandparents and it was important to transfer them."

J., a long-term immigrant from England who currently resides in Antwerp, sent her children to a non-Jewish school in the city, although she says it is not customary to do so among families where both parents are Jewish:

> Let's say people who aren't religious who feel very Jewish and traditional, nobody would ever think of sending their children when they're young to a non-Jewish school, which is very strange because if you're not religious why not? We did, we sent our children to local schools. Didn't send them to a Jewish school but that's highly unusual here when both parents are Jewish. That will happen if one of the parents isn't Jewish because they're very strict on accepting a child where, well yeah, one parent isn't Jewish, if the mother isn't Jewish.

Y., who is long-term immigrant from Israel, born in Libya and residing in Antwerp, spoke about Judaism being important in the education of children:

> I think it is very important to teach children their place. It is very important to give the foundation. To study in a Jewish school is also [learning] secular science. It simply gives them a perspective on Judaism. We also learn about the Holocaust and everything that happened, and in any case this gives something to the children, to understand how important it is to be a Jew.

G., an emissary teacher from Israel, a religious woman who teaches in a local Jewish-Zionist school, noted that her children study in another Jewish school, which is more religious, and allows her children to enjoy the lifestyle to which they are accustomed:

> There was a very, very difficult deliberation, accompanied by an expectation from the school that our children would enter here, as [it would be] more suitable for us. [. . .] If

the children here are not religious and then you know, they bring non-*Kosher* food, or parties are on Saturdays, it creates all kinds of frictions and difficulties.

7.5 Summary

This chapter focused on Jewish identity and identification among our respondents, comparing native-born and immigrants and by city of residence. Research participants are predominantly Jewish by birth and report on endogenic patterns of marriage – as a whole. However, when compared by city of residence, it is obvious that those who reside in Brussels have higher non-Jewish roots as well as higher percentages of intermarriage. These results correspond with previous studies, although they referred to all Jews in France and Belgium and not by city of residence (see, for example, DellaPergola and Staetsky, 2020; Graham, 2018). Comparison between native-born and immigrants did not yield any significant differences in this regard.

Israeli immigrants to Paris, most of whom are long-term immigrants, have transnational identity of Israel and France, although not of the same intensity. Those who reside in the city for more than fifteen years try to integrate but acknowledge that they will always be strangers and not fully assimilated – a status which they seem to get used to. Some used terms such as "I am not really here" or 'a guest' to express their segregation from the host society, to a certain extent. This acculturation strategy could be also characterized as 'individual assimilation' (see Cohen E. H., 2011); they have negative attitude toward their co-migrants, the diasporic group but have positive attitude toward host and origin countries. Moroccan immigrants, who arrived at least two decades earlier than the Israelis did, in their teens and without their families, have weaker transnational identification with their countries of origin, which remained mainly a childhood memory, and thus are more affiliated with France. They also have very strong attachment to Israel as part of their Jewish-ethnic identity, as was found in previous studies. The interesting findings are that most native-born express transnational identity with Israel, which is not expected, since France encourages loyalty to the French state alone (see also Graham, 2018).

It seems that interviewees from Brussels have different perceptions of 'home': While one immigrant feels 'at home' in Belgium more than in Israel, the other feels disconnected regarding his country of origin but emphasizes the place of Israel as part of his religious identity. The two native-born in Brussels did not identify with Belgium. They both have transnational identification either with Israel or feel indifference regarding Belgium versus other countries.

Interviewees from Antwerp elaborate regarding the meaning of 'home' to them – from a broader perception to a more concrete definition of national identification – mainly with Israel, including indifference to this feeling of home. Israelis, particularly those who reside in Antwerp for less than ten years, apparently refer to Israel not only as their beloved home, but also as an important part of their ethnic identity. It is interesting to note that although Israel is an important part of their ethnic identity and identification, none of the Israeli interviewees mentioned diasporic elements in that regard (for example, participating in Israeli organizations or activities in their current communities abroad).

Long-term immigrants from either Israel or England are more attached to Belgium and their attachment to Israel is weaker. It is interesting to note that the only native-born who refers to these issues seems to be the most detached from his country.

Native-born obviously have stronger local-national identity, compared with immigrants, due to their nativity, and Parisians stand out in this regard. However, this national identity, as a whole, is not very high. On the other hand, nativity or being a Parisian do not 'protect' from feelings as minority and thus, excluded. Some immigrants feel as minority as well, but to a lesser degree, particularly those who reside in Antwerp and came from Israel, where they had been part of the majority in recent years. In addition, men reported feeling as minority more than women did, maybe due their ethnic visibility wearing a *Kippah* or other Jewish attire.

Ethnic identification regarding Jewish practice among respondents in the present study is very high among Parisians, similarly to previous findings, to be followed by Antwerp and finally – Brussels. *Sephardi,* who comprise the majority primarily in Paris also seem to practice religion to a greater extent than do *Ashkenazi* (see also Fourquet, 2015), who mostly reside in the Belgian cities. It should also be noted that Paris is much larger than each of the Belgian cities and thus offers more Jewish services such as *Kosher* food, which might affect some of the results here, regarding Jewish practice. Nevertheless, the pattern of high ethnic identification among Jews in France – in general, and as this study indicates – Paris in particular, prove that a large portion of Jews in this city attach great importance to their Jewish identification. The two Belgian cities, although having Jewish facilities in both, differ in their Jewish identification; Antwerp is stronger in this regard, and Brussels is more secular. In addition, native-born tend to practice religion more than immigrants do. This could also explain the differences by cities, since in Antwerp and Brussels there are more immigrants (some came in the last six years or recently), while in Paris there are more native-born or long-term immigrants.

Chapter 8
Discussion: Two Jewish Communities in Three Cities - Challenges of Integration, Acculturation and Identity

8.1 Overview

This book, based upon questionnaires addressed to contemporary European Jews residing in three urban Jewish communities, Paris, Brussels and Antwerp, presents findings and discussions of interviews conducted with Jewish residents: More than half native-born and the rest - immigrants. The three communities share several traits in common, yet each is distinct in its Jewish residents' patterns of integration, acculturation strategies as well as ethnic identity vis-a-vis the non-Jewish majority, and differ between themselves.

Most importantly, contemporary interactions and inter-relations are also affected by the history of the two nations, French and Belgian, with regard to their Jewish communities. Different policy trajectories of France and Belgium, as well as those in the three cities, accompanied by characteristics of local non-Jewish native-born and immigrants, affect majority-minorities inter-relations, including local Jews. Jews in France and Belgium, when compared by three cities, also differ in numerous components regarding their socio-demographic and socio-economic characteristics, as well as their Jewish background. Most Paris residents define themselves as *Sephardi* while the same percentage of Jews residing in the Belgian cities consider themselves *Ashkenazi*. In Paris, and particularly in Brussels, the socio-economic status is high with regard to respondents' educational attainment and occupational prestige, whereas Antwerp Jews have the lowest status. In the three cities, socio-economic status is higher among the native-born. These findings partially result from upward mobility opportunities, more available to native-born than to immigrants. These differences also originate in the structure of the local Jewish community itself as well as in the unique fabric of the city of residence: Its size, policy towards minorities and immigrants and cultural diversity.

Native-born and long-term immigrants (more than 15 years since immigration) differ from immigrants, particularly from those recently arrived from Israel, in their perceptions, patterns of integration as well as acculturation and ethnic identity. Daily interactions among Jews as privileged minorities and the majority create unique patterns of attachments which, for some, are local-national, assimilative or local-communal and entail segregation from the non-

https://doi.org/10.1515/9783110698817-008

Jewish; for others, they enhance more transnational ties, either with Israel or other countries.

Nonetheless, city of residence is the most powerful factor which enables the most comprehensive understanding of inter-relations between Jews and non-Jews in contemporary Western Europe and in tracing different trajectories regarding Jewish vitality and continuity.

Since representative socio-demographic and socio-economic data regarding Jews in France and Belgium are not obtainable, the importance of the study this book offers lies firstly in the quantitative data it supplies. Although some data correspond with previous surveys of Jewish communities, data presented in this book focus on a comparison of three cities and between native-born and immigrants, which, to my knowledge, has not been studied yet. The innovation of this study is in its detailed description of updated socio-demographic attributes of age, gender, occupation, educational level, dwelling ownership, ethnic origin affiliation and country of origin, in a comparison between native-born residents and immigrants, and of the three cities. The study also dwells on dispersal trajectories in the three cities, stemming from Jewish community and continuity tendencies as well as changes in Jewish residents' socio-economic status. These comparisons elaborate and enrich knowledge regarding Jews in these two countries in a more specific and thorough manner than published so far.

Though referring extensively to rising antisemitism as well as xenophobic incidents, very noticeable and widely reported in contemporary Europe, this book foregrounds a comprehensive analysis of challenges, strengths, vitality, dynamics and continuity of these three Jewish communities, including their native-born, old and new immigrants.

These common traits as well as differences are discussed according to three themes: 1) Integration, segregation and assimilation within the non-Jewish majority; 2) Jewish communal continuity and vitality; 3) Multiple ethnic identity and identification: Strengths and challenges.

8.2 Integration and Acculturation to the Non-Jewish Majority

When asked to describe inter-relations between Jewish and non-Jewish communities in the three cities from macro perceptions, most interviewees attend negatively to new Muslim immigrants, who are definitely more present in Paris and Brussels. Some of these attitudes are evidence-based on recent terror attacks, and some on stereotypes, based upon islamophobia that became a common characteristic of Europe. In Antwerp and in Brussels there are also other new immigrants who came from more similar cultures to the European ones, such as workers in EU offices or those from a higher socio-economic status; thus, they are described as less intimidating and more favorable, although not entirely welcome by the Belgian host society. Immigrants who arrived in earlier decades (fifties to seventies, primarily) are perceived as more integrated and less religious, Muslims included, both in Paris and in Brussels. Interviewees' nostalgic perceptions of French, and to some extent, Belgian society as having equal and plural policies towards Jews and other former colonial residents, seem to contradict the negative feelings, including fear, resulting from recent reconstruction of inter-relations.

Personal integration within the majority is evident mainly in economic and occupational mobility opportunities, and thus involves successful integration as a whole. However, Parisians and those from Antwerp, particularly immigrants, are more segregated from the majority in these cities both socially and culturally, whereas assimilation is more prevalent among Brussels' native-born residents. It seems that separation is more voluntary and not due to overt exclusion policies towards Jews - native-born or immigrant - regardless of city of residence. Thus, allegedly, Jews in this study seem to have a large range of choices with regard to their integration and acculturation strategies to the majority, encouraged by French and Belgian policies towards ethnic minorities and immigrants.

Nevertheless, respondents, particularly those from Paris and Brussels express a quite recent sense of alienation and even fear; this contradicts the picture of allegedly successful integration within the majority. These feelings are partially reflected in predisposition to emigrate elsewhere and might explain patterns of socio-cultural segregation or separation, which were described earlier. Surprisingly, native-born, who are more integrated in the majority, are those who are more predisposed to emigrate, while immigrants are more reluctant to re-migrate. A possible explanation for these findings is that immigrants, particularly those who came more than a decade ago to France, made efforts to integrate. These efforts are mentioned by some in the interviews. Short-term immigrants, particularly Israelis, did not fulfill their aspirations through immigration yet, and thus, also do not talk or report on their wishes to emigrate.

Thus, each community of Jews, native-born and immigrants, is subject to different socio-cultural, economic opportunities and policy towards minorities and immigrants in its city of residence. These relationships effect patterns of integration within the majority as well as the choosing acculturation strategies. Although France and Belgium enable and declare equal and liberal opportunities for integration, daily interactions between Jews - although as privileged minorities - seem to limit some, and create new boundaries of segregation and separation from the majority. Some of these xenophobic and racist manifestations towards minorities and immigrants in Europe as a whole, and towards

Jews in particular, are overt, and some are subtler when expressed in 'new' and 'old' antisemitic acts.

Acceleration of antisemitism in everyday life is felt by Jews in Paris, both native-born and long-term immigrants, although from slightly different angles: While those from the first group acknowledge 'old' antisemitism as well as 'new' one, immigrants from Maghreb countries, or even Israel, blame it particularly on new or second-generation Muslim immigrants. These differences possibly stem from countries of origin, which may have affected the respondents' acquaintance either with Christian-native-born or with Muslims. This pattern also characterizes native-born interviewees and long-term immigrants from Brussels and Antwerp. They can detect hidden or subtler manifestations of antisemitism among the non-Jewish majority, whereas recent immigrants from Israel are either unaware of antisemitism or attribute it to Muslims. As mentioned earlier, antisemitic manifestations create feelings of fear, alienation and predisposition for future emigration, particularly among those who are supposedly affiliated and safe in their countries of birth and cities of residence.

The contribution of this study is in elaborating theories regarding integration of minorities and immigrants within the majority in multiple areas: Economic, social, communal and cultural. Integration patterns and acculturation strategies should be analyzed as dynamic and complemental and dynamic; while in one area integration is more prevalent, in others it could be partial and changing over-time. Macro and micro perceptions, feelings and attitudes, regarding national and local city of residence, apparent in the questionnaires or interviews, reflect currently modified interactions, deriving from new national and local policies as well as local population change. Those who previously felt part of the majority, now may express feelings of exclusion, segregation or even separation. Furthermore, the comparison of three cities and between immigrants and native-born, deepens understanding of the dynamics along the time-line, and facilitates comprehension of current events of inter-relations between Western Europe Jews and the majority. Jews, who consisted a privileged included minority within pluralistic, multi-cultured and liberal societies, have become gradually excluded in the last decades and turned into 'Others' - overtly and subtly.

8.3 Jewish Communal Continuity and Vitality

Demographic and ethnic changes the three Jewish communities have undergone, point to three main trajectories that characterize the organizational, vital and denominative structure of each city. The ethnic and demographic structure of Parisian Jewish community changes in a very significant pattern - from mostly

Ashkenazi to mostly North African - first and second-generation immigrants. Thus, the organizational and denominative character of this community expanded but went through metamorphosis from a secular-liberal and more assimilative community to a strong and cohesive Jewish community and thus more segregated from the host society. Brussels' Jewish community remained *Ashkenazi* and liberal; most of the more Orthodox emigrated elsewhere, and the local community has fewer synagogues or other religious Jewish institutions. However, there is an alternative trajectory which is expressed in educational systems such as Jewish schools (not many but very active and popular) and youth movements, and in donations to the Jewish community. Involvement in education and donations give the community a vibrant essence, although may not prevent assimilation in the near future. Finally, in Antwerp, the same ethnic Jewish community remained *Ashkenazi*; however, the younger generations are more religious and even ultra-Orthodox. Accordingly, previous Jewish denominations shrank, and new Jewish organizations, as well as educational institutions emerged.

Compared to the past, the Parisian Jewish community appears much stronger and vital in the last three decades, regarding not only the older generation but youngsters as well. Religion became more significant in everyday life, synagogues expanded in numbers and in their centrality, *Kosher* food is more available; the Hebrew language as well as restaurants became more prominent. However, findings of the present study confirm a previous one; since state education is considered the key to national identity, and Jewish schools are costly, Parisians send their children primarily to non-Jewish schools and to a lesser extent than those from Belgian cities. The Parisian Jewish community strengthened and supported immigrants who came primarily from North Africa and who became the successors of *Ashkenazi*, mostly secular residents. Parisians also reported higher intermarriage with other Jews from their Jewish community than did the Belgians - which indicates that Jews in Paris keep stronger ingroup religious connections.

Interviews indicate that Brussels is a city with *Ashkenazi* majority, but primarily secular and liberal. Brussels has a Jewish community which seems to be the most secular in comparison with Paris and Antwerp, but a large portion of parents send their children to Jewish schools, which are funded by the government. Those who are ultra-Orthodox prefer to emigrate to Antwerp or at least send their children to study there. Brussels Jews seem to maintain their Jewish community through community organizations with a more secular orientation such as youth movements (few but very popular), Jewish schools with Zionist and less religious orientation, as well as other cultural-communal activities.

Antwerp is also mostly *Ashkenazi*-origin community, which was once secular and recently became ultra-Orthodox and thus constitutes a visible Jewish minority. Although there are some small communities of Moroccan Jews (old-term immigrants) and Georgian Jews, who arrived to Antwerp in the last decade; they have their own communities and organizations. The only common and uniting component of all these Jewish communities is working in the diamond industry, which is in decline anyway since the economic crisis of 2008. Other than that, they seem to be separate regarding their denomination, religiosity, ethnic origins and interests: Native-born, long-term and short-term immigrants (less than 15 years after immigration). While the ultra-Orthodox impact on the strength and vitality of the local Jewish community, including the revival of its organizations, *Ashkenazi* secular native-born Jews became marginal to the community in a similar pattern to Paris' *Ashkenazi* group. In addition, Antwerp's local *Ashkenazi* religious-Zionist and *Sephardi* communities are small and less significant than the ultra-Orthodox with regard to the organizational and educational structure within the local Jewish community.

Analysis of social networks and their structure could indicate local communities' degree of coherence, implying whether inter-relations are loose or tight. In this regard, immigrant respondents seem to have more transnational connections (particularly with Israel) and diasporic connections, with immigrants from their country of origin, regardless of the years they reside in the city. Some also mentioned friends from work. The few native-born who responded to this question of 'close friends' either have very few, or mention Jewish friends and family as their close friends. Some refer to being left alone after their friends emigrated from the country. Some immigrants, as well as native-born interviewees, described their social networks as comprised of local non-Jewish friends, too. Parisians tend more toward ethno-social segregation than do Jews in Belgian cities, particularly in Brussels, who have higher tendency towards assimilation. Those residing in Antwerp, some immigrants themselves (particularly Israelis), have diasporic social networks, similar to those from Paris, but with more emphasis on transnational networks - with friends and family in Israel.

Thus, with regard to Jewish communal, organizational and social vitality, qualitative as well as quantitative data in this study provide new and updated results. Not only does the majority society affect continuity and strength of each community; also, inner demographic, socio-economic and ethnic changes dynamically reconstruct new religious, educational or other local Jewish organizations, while degenerate others. Although the size of each city and its socio-communal structure are different, it is primarily the Jewish community and the changing composition of its members and the tightness of formal and informal social network that affect their vitality and continuity. These findings employ and elaborate on theoretical terms of communal organizations - both secular and religious, formal and informal. They also expand understanding of social networks, their structure - whether local, diasporic, assimilative or transnational. Inter-relations among these terms are different not only by city of residence but also between native-born and particularly immigrants.

8.4 Cultural Integration within Jewish Communities: Ethnic Identity and Acculturation

This study includes predominantly participants who are Jewish by birth and who have endogenic patterns of marriage. However, when compared to Paris and Antwerp, those who reside in Brussels have higher rate of non-Jewish roots as well as percentages of intermarriage, in consistence with other findings in this study, whereas Brussels' Jewish residents are more prone to economic and mainly to socio-cultural integration and sometimes - assimilation to the majority. Native-born and immigrants are quite similar in this regard.

Feeling 'at home' could indicate communal affiliation and identity as locals, minorities or immigrants. For example, for most long-term immigrants, transnational identity is common, either with Israel or other countries of origin. However, some also mentioned, at different levels of intensity, their alienation from their city of residence and feelings of exclusion as minorities and immigrants. Immigrants from Maghreb countries to Paris, who are mostly old-term immigrants, have weaker transnational identity and thus are more affiliated and feel at 'home' in their city of residence. Yet, interestingly, similarly to most native-born Jews of France, they also feel very strong attachment to Israel as part of their Jewish identity. Native-born French Jews' attachment is, however, unexpected since France encourages national loyalty alone.

Brussels' and Antwerp's Jewish residents expressed lesser national identity than those from Paris, those from Brussels are more diffused in their transnational identities, including native-born. Immigrants in the Belgian cities can be characterized as experiencing 'nostalgic separation'; they have more negative attitude toward the host culture but positive and nostalgic attitude toward their co-migrants, and countries of origin. Thus, Brussels interviewees are mostly segregated or separated regarding their socio-cultural integration within the majority. Multiple-hyphenated identities characterize mainly immigrants, but also native-born who describe their dynamic shifts from one identity to another along their lives in interaction with the host society. Their multiple identities sometimes 'clash' and sometimes only change in the course of time.

Jewish practice which reflects on ethnic identification is very high among Parisians, to be followed by Antwerp and finally - Brussels. Although there are differences in religious services which each city can offer due to its size, the vitality of the three Jewish communities originates in their Jewish residents and the importance they attach to religious practice, as mentioned earlier in this chapter, regarding Jewish organizations. In the interviews, confirmed by quantitative data, *Sephardi* residents in Paris attribute very high importance to their Jewishness, unlike their parents and primarily *Ashkenazi* Parisians. Thus, Jewish organizations and practices have been on the rise in the last decades. The two Belgian cities are more *Ashkenazi* and less interested in the religious component of their Jewish being, particularly in Brussels. The change in the Jewish community in Antwerp, as mentioned earlier, and the rise of the *Haredi* (ultra-Orthodox) subcommunity strengthened religious organizations and services in the city, which otherwise might gradually vanish. Short-term Jewish immigrants, particularly those who reside in the Belgian cities (especially Israelis) contribute to formal and informal educational institutions and generally help to maintain Jewish practice and services but do not change them, so that native-born incline to practice religion more than immigrants do in the three cities.

Another expression of Jewish identification is Jewish socialization and education of respondents' children. Regardless of city of residence, immigrants and native-born, seem to want Jewish socialization for their children in order to preserve their Jewish identity and attachment to Israel. For secular Jews keeping their children in Jewish educational systems is a greater challenge, since some are married to non-Jewish spouses. Religious participants have more avenues to maintain their children's Jewish identification. Even if their denomination demands stricter or lighter Jewish education they find what they need, particularly in between the two Belgian communities. Nevertheless, even in Brussels, where the Jewish community is much more secular and liberal, they can maintain their children's Jewish socialization through Jewish, though less religious schools and youth movements.

These findings expand on other studies which compare France and Belgium as a whole and not by city of residence, and do not distinguish between native-born or immigrants. It seems that each community has its own challenges versus strength, vitality and potential for continuity. Multiple dynamic Jewish ethnic identity and identification are parts of these challenges and strengths. Demographic and ethnic changes in each city, short-term and long-term immigrants, and their inter-relations with native-born, construct and reconstruct Jewish community religious services or other organizations which enable Jewish practice and education. These changes and impact acculturation strategies within the three Jewish communities, as well as to the majority. Israel constitutes a significant and central part of Jewish identity and identification, for both immigrants and native-born in the three cities, serving as a spiritual stronghold as well as homeland and concrete option for future migration.

Furthermore, there are significant correlations resulting from quantitative data that elaborate the scope of the relationship between Jewish identity and patterns of integration and acculturation: Those who report on high degree of Jewish identity, strong attachment with Israel, are the ones who tend to practice religion, feel rather integrated within the local Jewish community, have mainly Jewish friends and are less prone to assimilation to the non-Jewish majority. Thus, strong ethnic identity and frequent religious practice contribute to in-group cohesiveness, tighter social networks and resilience. However, it creates segregation from the out-group, the majority, particularly in socio-cultural spheres, as evident particularly in Paris.

Nevertheless, some sectors in each community still face challenges of assimilation and exclusion. In addition, national attachment to France and Belgium is particularly sensitive and questionable these days, with the rise of antisemitism. However, it seems that all three communities find their unique opportunities to maintain their existence, by recruiting their internal powers, native-born and immigrants, in accord with multiple contemporary manifestations of Jewish identity and identification, as well as by coping with the majority.

8.5 Policy Trajectories and Further Research

Contemporary Jewish communities in France and Belgium are significant on their own and important to world Jewry, as a whole; the French Jewish community is third in size and the Belgian is the 16th. These communities are composed mainly of native-born but also of old-term and recent immigrants. Demographic considerations of emigration from France and Belgium, as a result of different push motives, including the rising rate of antisemitism, should attract attention to policy considerations. These policy trajectories include three main components: 1) Each community and its inner ethnic diversity and structure as well as inter-relations among the three Jewish communities; 2) Interactions with national and local non-Jewish communities and policies, including native-born and immigrants; 3) Israel as homeland and spiritual center as well as source of support and potential for future immigration.

As shown in this study, the three Jewish communities have resilience and strength to remain strong Jewish communities that can resist antisemitism rising in the last two decades. Jews in the three communities are mostly well integrated, particularly economically and professionally. It seems that for most of them segregation from the majority regarding social, cultural, religious and ethnic identity is voluntary. However, some challenges cannot be ignored. Ethnic and demographic changes are evident in all three communities, as a result of age, birth rates, immigration and emigration. Paris' community became more coherent and religious but particularly for the younger generation and mainly for *Sephardi*. Other groups of secular and *Ashkenazi* origin are excluded, although not intentionally. Policy focusing on those who are not of the main stream might strengthen the community, which also faces another challenge of constant emigration to other European countries, the Unites States and of course - Israel. Those who emigrate are from average or upper socio-economic status, including young people; this is a considerable challenge which the Jewish community in Paris should address. Emigration is also connected to possible inter-relations with Belgian Jewish communities that confront different challenges.

Brussels' Jewish community is famous for its liberal attitudes and policies, as also evident in this study. Brussels offers international opportunities and attracts many recent immigrants from high socio-economic status, Israelis included. Brussels' community has its strength with regard to its Jewish formal and informal liberal-Zionist-secular education, in whose implementation Israelis participate. In this regard, Paris' and Brussels' communities complement each other, since most Parisian children do not attend Jewish schooling or informal educational frames. Paris has numerous other options which can attract Jewish youth from Brussels, to take part in Jewish activities. Brussels' Jewish community is the most prone to assimilation and thus mutual collaboration between the two French speaking communities could benefit both.

Antwerp has become more strictly religious than Paris, although the majority are still *Ashkenazi*; but, similarly to Paris, they feel excluded, this time due to their secularity. There are short-term immigrants in Antwerp but each group has almost no connection with the other. Thus, policy to integrate the various groups in Antwerp and share Jewish educational and religious structure can strengthen the community. Cooperation with Brussels' Jewish community seems loose as well, and exists mainly on the educational level, whereas ultra-Orthodox Jews from Brussels send their children to study in Antwerp.

The two Belgian communities, although adjacent geographically and linguistically seem to draw apart from each other; whereas one is secular, liberal but has obvious community coherence and activities, the other changes dramatically but with almost no common community organizations which can unite immigrants and native-born from multiple religious affiliations or even secular Jews. Due to linguistic differences and the diffuseness of Antwerp's Jewish community, it seems that in the short-term, cooperation between Antwerp and Paris is hard to achieve, even though the two communities have similar high Jewish identity and identification and could benefit each other on a common religious ground. Paris-Brussels' and Brussels-Antwerp' policies of cooperation seem more realistic, at least these days. The three communities reside and function in non-Jewish states, which are predominantly Christian but also have high percentages of Muslim population, particularly in Paris and Brussels. Although France and Belgium have liberal and equal policies towards ethnic minorities and immigrants, part of which are implemented in the three cities, 'new' antisemitism as well as other xenophobic manifestations are in constant rise, including during the COVID-19 pandemic (although with fewer violent attacks due to lock-downs).

Evidently from interviews and questionnaires presented in this study, Jews in Paris and Brussels reported on their feelings of fear and alienation from their cities of residence, including native-born and long-term immigrants. Some also reported on their predisposition to emigrate and join others who had already left the country. France and Belgium are changing, demographically and ethnically; former multicultural, liberal and equal rights undergo ongoing 'withdrawal.' Thus, it is extremely important that Jewish communities' leadership act together in order to fight antisemitism which became an everyday occurrence. As I argued here, the cohesiveness of the local Jewish community, inter-relations and cooperation of the three communities can create a leadership which will affect policy changes towards Jews in particular, and other minorities. in general. Finally, Israel that serves as an imaginary community for some, a spiritual center or a destination country for immigration for others, has responsibility for keeping these communities strong and vivid.

Although some policies in the past yielded formal and informal educational projects for children and youth through emissaries and Israeli teachers, they are fewer than those in North America. Evidently from this study, the three communities have their own institutions; however, each city can benefit from more diverse Jewish educational institutions aimed at plural Jewish affiliations. Israel can also be more involved in supporting Jews in France and Belgium, particularly by firmer fight against rising antisemitism.

These conclusions may lead to further research, based on mixed methods, which can be conducted in other urban Jewish communities in Europe or elsewhere, focusing on the three dimensions elaborated here. The first may analyze inter-relations and components of integration into the majority both national and local, including changes in policy and scope of antisemitism - 'old' or 'new.' The second dimension may focus on inner Jewish communal continuity and vitality as a result of demographic changes, such as short-term immigrants and emigrants versus old-term immigrants and native-born Jews, and the reconstruction of community institutions.

Finally, further study may compare patterns and dynamics of multiple cultural integration and acculturation, ethnic identity and identification, and explore the place of Israel in supporting inner Jewish communities' strengths and resilience. By comparing contemporary Jewish communities, we can further understand each one's characteristics, strengths as well as weaknesses and suggest collaborations between themselves as well as with local, national and international organization and states, in which Israel has an important role.

This study demonstrates that the three communities of Paris, Brussels and Antwerp have strength and vitality of their own, which predict their scope of continuity in the future. However, inner changes of population, structure of organizations, ethnic identity and affiliations, accompanied by interactions on daily basis with the non-Jewish majority call for new collaborations and policy trajectories beyond the single Jewish community.

List of Tables

https://doi.org/10.1515/9783110698817-009

References

Abitbol, M., and A. Astro. "The Integration of North African Jews in France." *Yale French Studies* 85 (1994): 248–261.

Abugov, N. and S. Gillis. "Nominal Plurals in Antwerp Hasidic Yiddish: An Empirical Study." *Linguistics* 54 (6) (2016):1397–1415.

Adam, I. *Les Entités Fédérées Belges et l'Intégration des Immigrés*. Editions de l'Université de Bruxelles, 2013.

American Jewish Committee (AJC). "AJC Survey on Antisemitism in France." *American Jewish Committee (AJC)*, 2020. Accessed April 24, 2021. https://www.ajc.org/news/ajc-paris-survey-french-jews-non-jews-agree-on-scope-of-antisemitism

Alidadi, K., M. Foblets, and J. Vrielink, eds. *A Test of Faith? Religious Diversity and Accommodation in the European Workplace*. Ashgate Publishing, 2012.

Avenarius, C. B. "Migrant Networks in New Urban Spaces: Gender and Social Integration." *International Migration* 50 (5) (2012): 25–55.

Barak, M. "Native-Born Minority/ Homeland Minority." Center for Educational Technology, 2006. (Hebrew).

Basch, L. G., N. Glick-Schiller, and C. B. Szanton. *Nation Unbound: Transnational Projects, Postcolonial Predicaments and Deterritorialized Nation States*. Gordon and Breach, 1994.

Bauman, Z. "Allosemitism: Premodern, Modern, Postmodern." In *Modernity, Culture, and 'The Jew,'* edited by B. Cheyette and L. Marcus, 143–156. Stanford University Press, 1998.

Bauman, Z. *Community: Seeking Safety in an Insecure World*. Cambridge Polity Press, 2001.

Beit Hatfutsot. *Paris*. Beit Hatfutsot, 1996. Accessed January 25, 2021.https://dbs.bh.org.il/place/paris.

Ben-Rafael, E. "Belgian Jews and Neo- Antisemitism." *Contemporary Jewry* 37 (2) (2017): 275–293.

Benea P., and M. Emmanuel. "Migrants Driving Cities' Development Agenda: The Importance of Including Migration in Urban Planning." IOM, 2015. Accessed April 14, 2020. https://weblog.iom.int/migrants-driving-cities-development-agenda-importance-including-migration-urban-planning

Bensimon, D., and S. DellaPergola. *La Population Juive de France: Socio-Demographie et Identite*. Hebrew University of Jerusalem, 1984.

Berry, J. W. "Immigration, Acculturation, and Adaptation." *Applied Psychology* 46 (1) (1997): 5–34.

Berry, J. W. "A Psychology of Immigration." *Journal of Social Issues* 57 (2001): 615–631.

Berry, J. W. "Acculturation: Living Successfully in Two Cultures." *International Journal of Intercultural Relations* 29 (2005): 697–712.

Boyd, M. "Family and Personal Networks in International Migration: Recent Developments and New Agendas." *International Migration Review* 23 (3) (1989): 638–670.

Brodkin, K. *How Jews Became White Folks and What That Says About Race in America*. Rutgers University Press, 1998.

Castles, S., and M. J. Miller. *The Age of Migration: International Population Movements in the Modern World*. Macmillan, 2009.

Castles, S., H. de Haas, and M. J. Miller. *The Age of Migration: International Population Movements in the Modern World*. Guilford Press, 2014.

https://doi.org/10.1515/9783110698817-010

Chini, M. "Belgium's Effective Retirement Age Lowest in All OECD Countries." *The Brussels Times*, 27 November, 2019. Accessed March 12, 2021. https://www.brusselstimes.com/brussels/129341/brussels-public-transport-runs-at-full-capacity-again-as-schools-reopen/

Chiswick, B. R. "The Effect of Americanization on the Earnings of Foreign-Born Men." Journal *of Political Economy* 86 (5) (1978): 897–921. Accessed July 12, 2021. http://www.jstor.org/stable/1828415.

Christiansen, C. C. "News Media Consumption among Migrants in Europe: The Relevance of Diaspora." *Ethnicities* 4 (2) (2004): 185–207.

Cohen, E. H. *The Jews of France at the Turn of the Third Millennium: A Sociological and Cultural Analysis*. The Rappaport Center for Assimilation Research and Strengthening Jewish Vitality, Bar Ilan University, 2009.

Cohen, E. H. "Impact of the Group of Co-Migrants on Strategies of Acculturation: Towards an Expansion of the Berry Model." *International Migration* 49 (4) (2011): 45–62.

Cohen, E. H. *France*. In *Perceptions and Experiences of Antisemitism among Jews in Selected EU Member States*, edited by D. Staetsky, J. Boyd, E. Ben-Rafael, E. Cohen, S. DellaPergola, L. Dencik, O. Glöckner, and A. Kovács, 95–97. JPR/Institute for Jewish Policy Research and Ipsos MORI, 2013.

Cohen, E. H., and M. Ifergan. *Les Juifs de France: Valeurs et Identité*. Fonds Social Juif Unifié, 2003.

Cohen, M. "Les Juifs de France. Modernité et Identité." *Vingitème Siècle, Revu d'Histoire Religions d'Europe* 66 (2000): 91–106.

Cohen, Y. "Israeli-Born Emigrants: Size, Destinations and Selectivity." *IJCS: International Journal of Comparative Sociology* 52 (1–2) (2011): 45–62.

Creswell, J. W. *Research Design: Qualitative, Quantitative and Mixed Methods Approaches*. Sage, 2014.

Cunningham, H. and J. M. Heyman. "Introduction: Mobilities and Enclosures at Borders." *Identities Studies in Culture and Power* 11 (2004): 289–302.

Dahan, I. "The Role of Spiritual Leadership in Shaping Collective Identity: The Case of the French Immigrant Community in Israel." *Hed Haulpan Hachadash* 104 (2015): 65–78. (Hebrew).

DellaPergola, S. "Intermarriage among the Jews in America: A Few Thoughts of a Non-American." *Gesher* 133 (1996): 7–23. (Hebrew).

DellaPergola, S. *Jewish Demographic Policies: Population Trends and Options in Israel and in the Diaspora*. The Jewish People Policy Institute, 2011a.

DellaPergola, S. "Jews in Europe: Demographic Trends Contexts and Outlooks." In *A Road to Nowhere? Jewish Experiences in Unifying Europe*, edited by J. H. Schoeps and O. Glockner, 3–34. Brill, 2011b.

DellaPergola, S. "World Jewish Population, 2016." In *The American Jewish Year Book*, edited by A. Dashefsky, S. DellaPergola, and I. M. Sheskin, 253–332. Springer, 2017.

DellaPergola, S. "World Jewish Population, 2018." In *The American Jewish Year Book, 2018*, edited by A. Dashefsky, and I. M. Sheskin, 361–452. Berman, Jewish DataBank, 2019.

DellaPergola, S. "World Jewish Population, 2019." In *The American Jewish Year Book, 2019*, edited by A. Dashefsky, and I. M. Sheskin, 263–356. Berman, Jewish DataBank, 2020a.

DellaPergola, S. "Jewish Perceptions of Antisemitism in the European Union, 2018: A New Structural Look." *Analysis of Current Trends in Antisemitism* 40 (2) (2020b): 1–86.

DellaPergola, S., and I. M. Sheskin,"Global Dispersion of Jews: Determinants and Consequences." In *The Changing World Religion Map: Sacred Places, Identities, Practices and Politics*, edited by S. B. Brunn, 1311–1343. Springer, 2015.

DellaPergola, S., and D. L. Staetsky. *Jews in Europe in the Turn of the Millennium: Population Trends and Estimates*. Institute for Jewish Policy Research, 2020.

Deveeshouwer, P., M. Sacco, and C. Torrekens, "Introduction et Conclusions." In *Bruxelles Villes Mosaïque. Entre Espaces, Diversités et Politiques*, edited by P. Devleeshouwer, M. Sacco, and C. Torrekens, 9–23, 189–194. Edition de l'Université de Bruxelles, 2015.

Dimentstein, M., and R. Kaplan. *The Israeli-European Diaspora: A Survey about Israelis Living in Europe*. UK: JDC International Center for Community Development and Machon Kehilot, 2017. Accessed April 14, 2020. https://scholar.google.co.il/scholar?q=The+Israeli-Euro pean+Diaspora:+A+survey+about+Israelis+living+in+Europe&hl=iw≈sdt=0≈vis=1&oi= scholart

Dinnie, E., and A. Fischer. "The Trouble with Community: How 'Sense of Community' Influences Participation in Formal, Community-Led Organizations and Rural Governance." *Sociologia Ruralis* 60 (1) (2020): 243–259.

Echikson, W. "Is There a Future for Jews in Europe?" *The Times of Israel*, 7 February, 2021. Accessed June 2, 2021. https://blogs.timesofisrael.com/is-there-a-future-for-jews-in-europe/

Ellemars, N., P. Kortekaas, and J.W.Ouwerkerk. "Self-Categorization, Commitment to the Group and Group Self-Esteem as Related but Distinct Aspects of Social Identity." *European Journal of Social Psychology* 29 (2–3) (1999): 371–389.

Eriksen, T. H. *Ethnicity and Nationalism: Anthropological Perspectives*. Pluto Press, 1993.

ESREA France. "What Percentages of French People Own Property? Rent Property?" ESREA France, 2016. Accessed April 15, 2021. https://englishspeakingrealestateagentsfrance.com/what-percentage-of-french-people-own-property-rent-property/

Everett, S. S. "The Many (Im)possibilities of Contemporary Algerian Judaites." In *Algeria: Nation, Culture and Transnationalism 1988–2015*, edited by P. Crowley, 63–80. Liverpool University Press, 2017.

Favell, A. *Free Movers in Brussels: A Report on the Participation and Integration of European Professionals in the City*. Institute for Political Sociology and Methodology, 2001.

Favell, A., M. Feldblum, and M. P. Smith. "Symposium: Mobility and Migration. The Human Face of Global Migration: A Research Agenda." *Society* 44 (2) (2007): 15–25.

Featherstone, M. "Public Life, Information Technology and the Global City: New Possibilities for Citizenship and Identity Formation." In *Identity and Social Change*, edited by J. E. Davis, 53–79. Transaction Publishers, 2000.

Ferro, A. "Desired Mobility or Satisfied Immobility? Migratory Aspirations among Knowledge Workers. *Journal of Education and Work* 19 (2) (2006): 171–200.

Florence, E. and M. Martiniello. "The Links Between Academic Research and Public Policies in the Field of Migration and Ethnic Relations: Selected National Case Studies." *International Journal on Multicultural Societies* 7 (1) (2005): 3–10.

Fourquet, J. (2015). *Enquête Auprès des Juifs de France*. Institut Français d'Opinion Publique (Ifop) pour la Fondation Jean Jaurès, Département Opinion et Stratégies d'Entreprise, 2015. Accessed April 15, 2021. https://www.ifop.com/wp-content/uploads/2018/03/883-1-document_file.pdf

FRA (European Union Agency for Fundamental Rights). "Survey on Discrimination and Hate Crime against Jews in the EU 2018." GESIS Datenarchiv, Köln. ZA7491 Datenfile Version 1.0.0. Accessed April 15, 2021. https://doi.org/10.4232/1.13264.

Geoffroy, C. "'Mobile' Contexts/ 'Immobile' Culture." *Language and Intercultural Communication* 4 (2007): 279–290.

Glick-Schiller, N. "Citizens in Transnational Nation-States: The Asian Experience. In *Globalization and the Asia-Pacific: Contested Territories*, edited by K. Olds, P. Dicken, P. F. Kelly, L. Kong, and H. W. Yeung, 202–218. Routledge, 1999.

Glick-Schiller, N., N. L. Basch, and C. B. Szanton."Transnationalism: A New Analytic Framework for Understanding Migration." *Annals of the New York Academy of Sciences* 645 (1992): 1–24.

Glick-Schiller, N. L. Basch, and C.B. Szanton, "From Migrant to Transmigrant: Theorizing Transnational Migration." *Anthropological Quarterly* 68 (1) (1995): 48–63.

Gold, S. J. *The Israeli Diaspora*. Routledge, 2002.

Gold, S. J. "Patterns of Adaptation among Contemporary Jewish Immigrants to the US. In *American Jewish Year Book* 116, edited by A. Dashefsky, and I. Sheskin, 3–43. Springer, 2016.

Graham, D. *European Jewish Identity: Mosaic or Monolith? An Empirical Assessment of Eight European Countries*. Report, Institute for Jewish Policy Research (JPR), 2018. Accessed April 12, 2021. http://archive.jpr.org.uk/object-eur183.

Gross, Z. "Power, Identity, and Organizational Structure as Reflected in Schools for Minority Groups: A Case Study of Jewish Schools in Paris, Brussels, and Geneva." *Comparative Education Review* 50 (4) (2006): 603–624.

Gsir, S. "Housing and Segregation of Migrants: Antwerp in Belgium" In *Integration Policies at the Local Level: Housing Policies for Migrants*, edited by H. Fassmann, and Y. Franz, 39–54. Austrian Academy of Sciences Press, 2016. doi:10.1553/ISR_FB036s39.

Hannam, K., M. Sheller, and J. Urry. "Editorial: Mobilities, Immobilities and Moorings." *Mobilities* 1 (1) (2006): 1–22.

Haug, B., G. M. Dann, and M. Mehmetoglu. "Little Norway in Spain: From Tourism to Migration." *Annals of Tourism Research* 34 (1) (2007): 202–222.

Hertz- Lazarowits R., M. Yosef-Meitav, A. Farah, and N. Zoabi. "Arabs and Jewish Students at the University of Haifa: Identity Maps Drawing within the Complex Israeli Political Context." *Studies in Education* 3 (2010): 126–155.

Hollifield, J. F. and T. K. Wong. "The Politics of International Migration: How Can We 'Bring the State Back In'?" In *Migration Theory: Talking Across Disciplines*, edited by C. B. Brettell, and J. F. Hollifield, 227–288. Routledge, 2015.

Horowitz, B. "New Frontiers: 'Milieu' and the Sociology of American Jewish Education." *Journal of Jewish Education* 74: s1 (2008): 68–81.

International Organization for Migration (IOM). *Migrants and Cities: New Partnerships to Manage Mobility. World Migration Report 2015*. International Organization for Migration (IOM), 2015. Accessed February 15, 2021. http://publications.iom.int/books/world-migration-report-2015-migrants-and-cities-new-partnerships-manage-mobility#sthash.OFstnNsn.dpuf

Jewish Virtual Library. *Paris, France*. Jewish Virtual Library, 2021. Accessed February 15, 2021. https://www.jewishvirtuallibrary.org/paris

Jikeli, G. "Explaining the Discrepancy of Anti-Semitic Acts and Attitudes in 21st Century France." *Contemporary Jewry* 37 (2017): 257–273.

Kantor Center. *Antisemitism World-Wide 2019 and the Beginning of 2020*. Tel Aviv University, Kantor Centre for the Study of Contemporary European Jewry, 2020. Accessed July 15, 2020. http://humanities.tau.ac.il/sites/humanities_en.tau.ac.il/files/media_server/hu manities/kantor/Kantor%20Center%20World-wide%20Antisemitism%20in%202019%20- %20Main%20findings.pdf

Kantor Center. *Antisemitism World-Wide 2020*. Tel Aviv University, Kantor Centre for the Study of Contemporary European Jewry, 2021. Accessed July 1, 2021. https://enhumanities.tau. ac.il/sites/humanities_en.tau.ac.il/files/media_server/Antisemitism%20World-wide% 202020.pdf

Kipnis, B. "Greater Tel Aviv as a World City: A Point on the Global Network and a Giant Head in the Israeli Space." In *Tel Aviv-Yafo: From a Garden Suburb to a World City*, edited by B. Kipnis, 227–260. Pardess, 2009. (Hebrew).

Kivisto, P. "Theorizing Transnational Immigration: A Critical Review of Current Efforts." *Ethnic and Racial Studies* 24 (4) (2001): 547–577.

Koser, K. "Introduction: International Migration and Global Governance." *Global Governance* 16 (2010): 301–315.

La Constitution Belge. *La Constitution Belge*. Service Affaires Juridiques et Documentation Parlementaire de la Chambre des Représentants D/2021/4686/02, 2021. Accessed July 9, 2021. https://www.dekamer.be/kvvcr/pdf_sections/publications/constitution/grond wetFR.pdf

Laguerre, M. S. *Global Neighborhoods: Jewish Quarters in Paris*, London, *and* Berlin, 117–136. State University of New York Press, 2008.

Lev Ari, L. "Social and Cultural Absorption of Israelis in the USA: Distinctions between Oriental and *Ashkenazi* Jews." *Pe'amim* (2005): 101–102, 221–250. (Hebrew).

Lev Ari, L. *Returning Home: Research on Former Israeli Migrants Returned to Israel*. Ministry of Absorption, 2006. (Hebrew).

Lev Ari, L. *The American Dream: For Men Only? Gender, Immigration and the Assimilation of Israelis in the United States*. LFB Scholarly Publishing LLC, 2008.

Lev Ari, L. "North Americans, Israelis or Jews? The Ethnic Identity of Immigrants' Offspring." *Contemporary Jewry* 32 (3) (2012): 285–308.

Lev Ari, L." Multiple Identities among Israeli Migrants in Europe." *International Journal of Jewish Education Research* 6 (2013): 29–67.

Lev Ari, L." Back Home: Return Migration, Gender, and Assimilation among Israeli Emigrants." In *Research in Jewish Demography and Identity*, edited by E. Lederhendler, and U. Rebhun, 241–261. Academic Studies Press, 2015.

Lev Ari, L., and N. Cohen. "Between the Homeland and the Diaspora: The *Tzofim* Youth Movement and Ethnic Identity Formation among Second Generation Israeli Migrants in the United States." *Megamot* 38 (3–4) (2012): 681–708. (Hebrew).

Lev Ari, L., and N. Cohen. "Acculturation Strategies and Ethnic Identity among Second-Generation Israeli Migrants in the United States." *Contemporary Jewry* 38 (3) (2018): 345–364.

Lev Ari, L., Y. Mansfeld, and D. Mittelberg, "Globalization and the Role of Educational Travel to Israel in the Ethnification of American Jews." *Tourism Recreation Research* 28 (3) (2003): 15–24.

Levitt, P., and B. N. Jaworsky. "Transnational Migration Studies: Past Developments and Future Trends." *The Annual Review of Sociology* 33 (2007): 129–56.

Levitt, P., and N. Glick-Schiller. "Conceptualizing Simultaneity: A Transnational Social Field Perspective on Society." *International Migration Review* 38 (3) (2004): 1002–1039.

Macionis, G. *Sociology*. The Open University, 1999. (Hebrew).

Massey, D. S., J. Arango, G. Hugo, A. Kouaouci, A. Pellegrino, and J. E. Taylor. "Theories of International Migration: A Review and Appraisal." *Population and Development Review* 19 (3) (1993): 431–466.

Medding, P. Y., G. A. Tobin, S. B. Fishman, and M. Rimor. "Jewish Identity in Conversionary and Mixed Marriages." *Jewish Sociological Papers* 92 (1992): 3–76.

Newby, H. "Foreword." In *Community Life: An Introduction to Local Social Relations*, edited by G. Crow and G. Allan, xi–xii. Routledge, 2013.

Nossiter, A. "Macron Scraps Proposal to Raise Retirement Age in France." *The New York Times*, 1 January, 2020. Accessed May 17, 2020. https://www.nytimes.com/2020/01/11/world/europe/france-pension-protests.html.

Plasseraud, Y. "National Minorities/ New Minorities: What Similarities and Differences in Contemporary Europe? *Essais*, 2010. Accessed June 17, 2020. https://doi.org/10.7202/1064037ar

Pohorils, Y. "Aliya on the Decline: The Jews in France Want to Immigrate but Hesitate.' *Ynet, Judaism*, 23 December, 2017. Accessed July 1, 2020. https://www.ynet.co.il/articles/0,7340,L-5060835,00.html. (Hebrew).

Portes, A., and R. G. Rumbaut. *Legacies: The Story of the Migrant Second-Generation*. University of California Press, 2001.

Rebhun, U. *Migration, Community, and Identification: Jews in Late 20th Century in America*. The Hebrew University, Magnes, 2001. (Hebrew).

Rebhun, U. "Migrant Acculturation and Transnationalism: Israelis in the United States and Europe Compared." *Journal for the Scientific Study of Religion* 53 (3) (2014): 613–635.

Rebhun, U., and L. Lev Ari. *American Israelis: Migration, Transnationalism, and Diasporic Identity*. Brill, 2010.

Rebhun, U., and I. Pupko. *Far But Home: Migration, Jewish Identification, and Attachment to Homeland among Israelis Abroad*. Hebrew University of Jerusalem, Israel Ministry of Immigration and Absorption, and the Jewish Agency for Israel, 2010. (Hebrew).

Robinson J., A. J. Scott, and P. J. Taylor. "Cities in Time and Space." In *Working, Housing: Urbanizing. Springer Briefs in Global Understanding*, edited by J. Robinson, A. J. Scott, and P. J. Taylor, 5–20. Springer, 2016. DOI: 10.1007/978-3-319-45180-0_2

Saeys, A., Y. Albeda, N. Van Puymbroeck, S. Oosterlynck, G. Verschraegen, and D. Dierckx. *Urban Policies on Diversity in Antwerp, Belgium*. University of Antwerp, Centre on Inequality, Poverty, Social Exclusion and the City, 2014. Accessed July 13, 2020. https://www.urbandivercities.eu/wp-content/uploads/2013/05/Urban-Policies-on-Diversity-in-Antwerp.pdf

Sagi, A. *Critique of Jewish Identity Discourse*. Bar Ilan University, Rappaport Center for Assimilation Research and Strengthening Jewish Vitality, 2002. (Hebrew).

Schuster, L. "The Continuing Mobility of Migrants in Italy: Shifting Between Places and Statuses." *Journal of Ethnic and Migration Studies* 31 (4) (2005): 757–774.

Sheffer, G. *Diaspora Politics: At Home Abroad*. Cambridge University Press, 2003.

Schreiber, J. P. "Les Juifs en Belgique: Une Présence Continue Depuis le XIIIe siècle: Les Cahiers de la Mémoire Contemporaine." *Bijdragen Tot de Eigentijdse Herinnering* (2) (2000): 13–37.

Staetsky, L. D., and S. DellaPergola. *Why European Jewish Demography?* Institute for Jewish Policy Research (JPR), 2019.

Staetsky, L. D. "Antisemitic Victimization of Jews in Europe." *European Union Agency for Fundamental Rights 2019*. Publications Office of the European Union, 2021.

Tandé, A. "Cibler (ou Non) les Populations d'Origine Etrangère? L'Action Publique Bruxelloise à Epreuve des Discriminations Ethno-Raciales en Matière d'Emploi." In *Bruxelles Villes Mosaique: Entre Espaces, Diversités et Politiques*, edited by P. Devleeshouwer, M. Sacco, and C. Torrekens, 9–23. Université Libre de Bruxelles, Institut de Sociologie, 2015.

Timmerman, C., N. Fadil, I. Goddeeris, N. Clycq, and K. Ettourki. "Introduction." In *Moroccan Migration in Belgium: More Than 50 Years of Settlement*, edited by C. Timmerman, N. Fadil, I. Goddeeris, N. Clycq, and K. Ettourki, 9–20. Leuven University Press, 2017.

United Nations. *Recommendations on Statistics of International Migration*. Department of Economic and Social Affairs, Statistic Division 58 (1) (1998): 9–10.

United Nations. *The International Migration Report 2015 (Highlights)*. Department of Economic and Social Affairs, Population Division, International Migration, 2016. Accessed June 17, 2020. http://www.un.org/en/development/desa/population/migration/publications/mi grationreport/docs/Migration_increase_digitalcard.png.

United Nations. *International Migration 2019 (Highlights)*. Department of Economic and Social Affairs, Population Division, 2020. Accessed June 2, 2021. https://www.un.org/develop ment/desa/pd/sites/www.un.org.development.desa.pd/files/files/documents/2020/ Jan/un_2019_internationalmigration_highlights.pdf

United Nations. *International Migration 2020 (Highlights)*. New York: Department of Economic and Social Affairs, Population Division, 2021. Accessed June 18, 2021. https://www.un. org/development/desa/pd/sites/www.un.org.development.desa.pd/files/files/docu ments/2020/Jan/un_2019_internationalmigration_highlights.pdf

Vertovec, S. "Conceiving and Researching Transnationalism." *Ethnic and Racial Studies* 22 (2) (1999): 447–462.

Vertovec, S. "Super-Diversity and its Implications." *Ethnic and Racial Studies* 30 (6) (2007): 1024–1054.

Vertovec, S. "Conceiving Transnationalism." In *The Creolization Reader-Studies in Mixed Identities and Cultures*, edited by R. Cohen, and P. Toninato, 266–277. Routledge, 2010.

Vollebergh, A. "The Other Neighbor Paradox: Fantasies and Frustrations of 'Living Together' in Antwerp." *Patterns of Prejudice 50* (2) (2016): 129–149. Accessed July 20, 2020. https:// doi.org/10.1080/0031322X.2016.1161957

Wikipedia. "Yellow Vest Movement, 2020." Accessed February 12, 2021. https://en.wikipedia. org/wiki/Yellow_vests_movement

Wistrich, R.S. "Towards the Endgame? The French Republic and Its 'Jewish Question.'" *Trauma and Memory* 3 (2) (2015): 52–61.

World Jewish Congress. *France,* 2020. Accessed February 2021. https://www.worldjewishcon gress.org/en/about/communities/FR

Wasserstein, B. *Vanishing Diaspora – the Jews in Europe Since 1945*. Penguin Books, 1996.

Webber, J. (ed). *Jewish Identities in the New Europe*. Littman Library of Jewish Civilization, 1994.

Yiftachel, O. "The Homeland and Nationalism." *Encyclopedia of Nationalism*, 359–383. Academic Press, 2001.

Xhardez, C. "The Integration of New Immigrants in Brussels: An Institutional and Political Puzzle." *Brussels Studies* 105 (2016): 1–19. Accessed December 11, 2020. http://file:/// C:/Users/Owner/Downloads/brussels-1434.pdf

Index

https://doi.org/10.1515/9783110698817-011